ROBOTICS IN MEDICINE

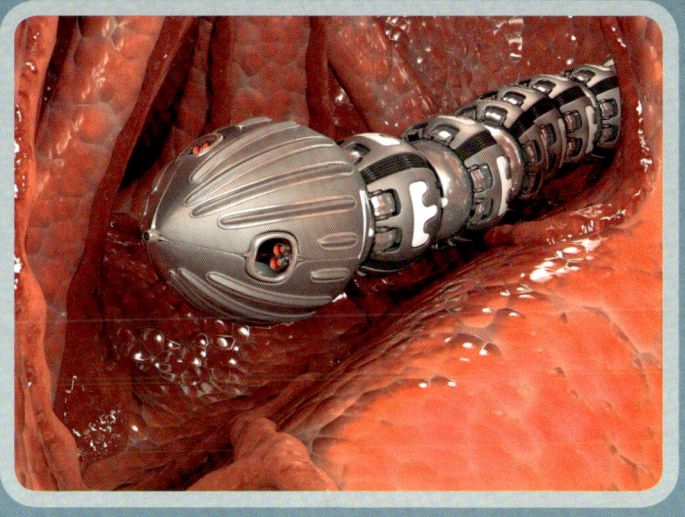

BY ROBYN HARDYMAN

LUCENT PRESS

Published in 2018 by
Lucent Press, an Imprint of Greenhaven Publishing, LLC
353 3rd Avenue
Suite 255
New York, NY 10010

Copyright © 2018 Lucent Press, an Imprint of Greenhaven Publishing, LLC.

All rights reserved. No part of this book may be reproduced in any form without permission in writing from the publisher, except by a reviewer.

Produced for Lucent Press by Calcium
Editors: Sarah Eason and Harriet McGregor
Designers: Paul Myerscough and Emma DeBanks
Picture researcher: Rachel Blount

Picture credits: Cover: ©2017 Intuitive Surgical, Inc.; Inside: ARxIUM 43; Carnegie Mellon University & University of Pittsburgh 33; Flickr: Aaron Biggs 34–35; ©2017 Intuitive Surgical, Inc. 14c, 14–15, 16–17, 17t, 46; John Hopkins University 11; Medrobotics Corporation 20, 21; Mazor Robotics, Inc. 12; Restoration Robotics, Inc. 22, 23; Prof. Sankai, University of Tsukuba/CYBERDYNE, INC. 28; Shutterstock: Agenturfotografin 44–45, Tewan Banditrukkanka 52–53, Olesia Bilkei 61t, Goran Bogicevic 48–49, Vereshchagin Dmitry 25, Iofoto 35t, Sebastian Kaulitzki 54–54, Liya Graphics 56–57, Max Margarit 5, Master Video 4, 13, Mehmetcan 10, Michaeljung 42–43, Monkey Business Images 29, MonstArr 52b, Mycteria 50–51, Nawin Nachiangmai 19, Tyler Olson 6, Racorn 26–27, Ramon Espelt Photography 32, Rocketclips, Inc. 45c, Rocksweeper 7, JC Roman 40t, Royaltystockphoto.com: 8–9, 38–39, Sergiy1975 55c, TaTae Thailand 49t, Tong2530 57t, Ververidis Vasilis 58b, Vectorfusionart 47, Vinne 36–37, Wavebreakmedia 40–41, Wire_man 1, 60–61, Zapp2Photo 58–59; SZI at Children's National Health Systems 18; Toyohashi University of Technology 31; Wikimedia Commons: Maggie Bartlett, National Human Genome Research Institute 50b, BLK Cyberkife Hospital, New Delhi, India 39b; Xenex Disinfection Services 8t.

Cataloging-in-Publication Data

Names: Hardyman, Robyn.
Title: Robotics in medicine / Robyn Hardyman.
Description: New York : Lucent Press, 2018. | Series: Robot pioneers | Includes index.
Identifiers: ISBN 9781534562097 (library bound) | ISBN 9781534562103 (ebook) | ISBN 9781534563025 (paperback)
Subjects: LCSH: Robotics in medicine--Juvenile literature. | Robots--Juvenile literature. | Medical technology--Juvenile literature. | Medical innovations--Juvenile literature.
Classification: LCC R857.R63 H369 2018 | DDC 610.285'63--dc23

Printed in the United States of America

CPSIA compliance information: Batch #CW18KL: For further information contact Greenhaven Publishing LLC, New York, New York at 1-844-317-7404.

Please visit our website, www.greenhavenpublishing.com. For a free color catalog of all our high-quality books, call toll free 1-844-317-7404 or fax 1-844-317-7405.

CONTENTS

Chapter 1 MEDICAL MARVELS 4

Chapter 2 SURGERY 10

Chapter 3 REHABILITATION AND MOBILITY 24

Chapter 4 NURSING AND WELL-BEING 28

Chapter 5 DELIVERING DRUGS 36

Chapter 6 TELEHEALTH 44

Chapter 7 RESEARCH AND DEVELOPMENT 48

Chapter 8 THE FUTURE 54

GLOSSARY 62

FOR MORE INFORMATION 63

INDEX 64

CHAPTER 1
MEDICAL MARVELS

Medicine is one of the great success stories of modern times. Over the past 100 years, so many amazing advances have been made in the understanding of diseases and the ability to treat them, that today people are living longer than ever before. Amazing advances in technology have been made, too. These have been combined with medical knowledge to help improve the healthcare people deliver. In recent years, one area of technology has begun to play a pioneering role in this process, and that is robotics.

Medicine is a highly skilled area of work. Medical practitioners train for many years to gain the skills they need to work safely and effectively with patients. However, in this field of expertise, robots have a pioneering role to play. As the population is getting older, and more people are seeking medical treatment, governments are facing huge challenges in meeting the cost of providing healthcare for all. Anything that can help to reduce costs, to keep people out of hospitals, or to enable doctors and nurses to spend more time with their patients has got to be welcomed.

Robots are working in so many different fields of medicine today. They are doing repetitive, time-consuming tasks such as dispensing medications in pharmacies and handling samples in research labs.

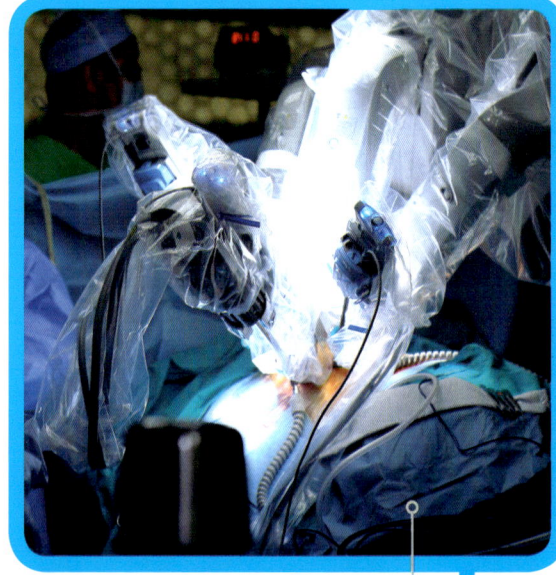

Robots and medical experts work together to improve healthcare.

4

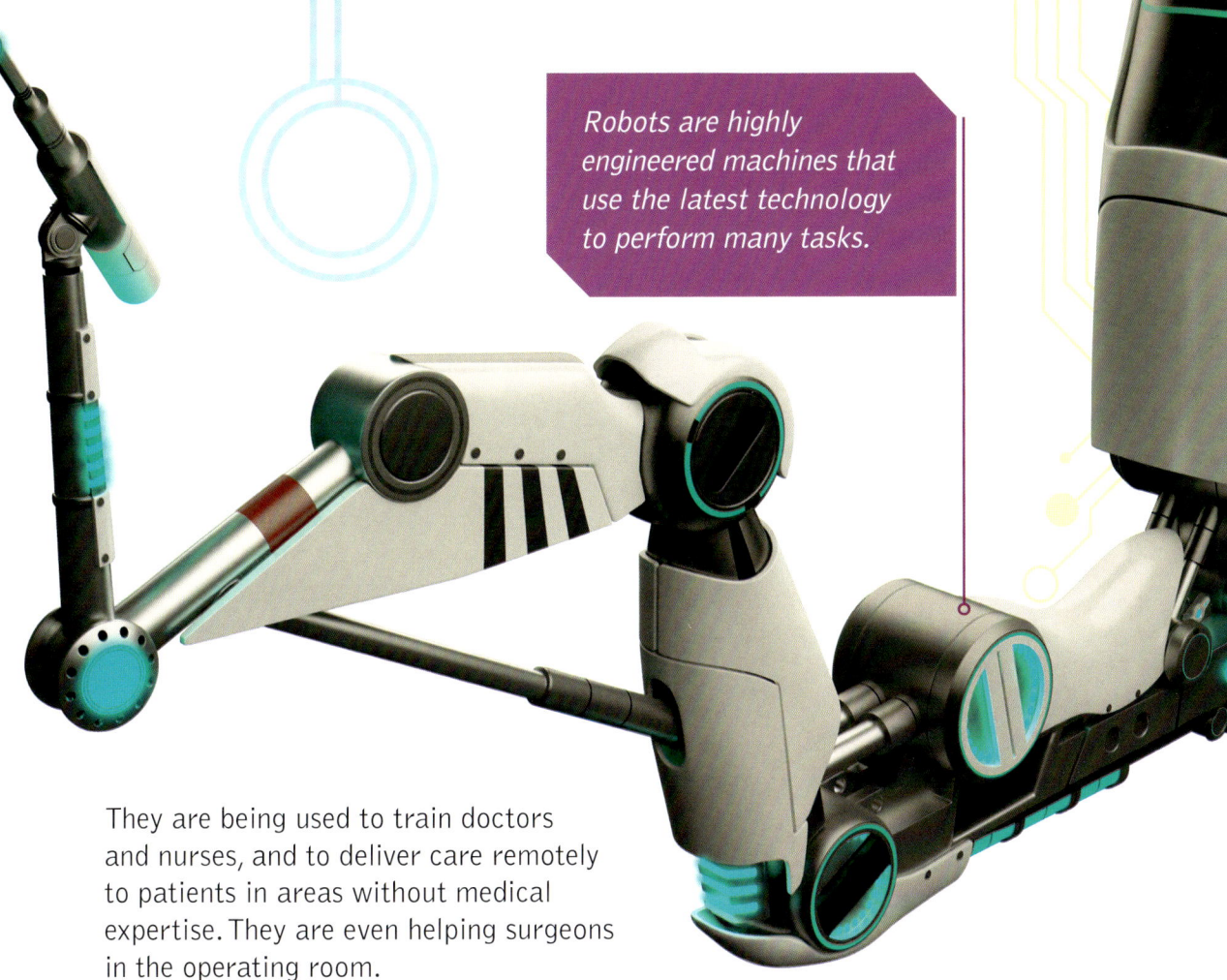

Robots are highly engineered machines that use the latest technology to perform many tasks.

They are being used to train doctors and nurses, and to deliver care remotely to patients in areas without medical expertise. They are even helping surgeons in the operating room.

What Is a Robot?

A robot is a machine that can be used to do a job. Some robots can do the job by themselves, with no human control. They are called autonomous. A robot on an assembly line in a car manufacturing plant is autonomous. It has been programmed to do its job without human intervention. Other robots must be controlled by a human. They can still do the task in some way better than a person, but they have controls that a person operates.

The use of robotics in medicine does raise some issues. These highly engineered machines are very expensive to buy and to maintain, so they must be shown to reduce costs in the long term. They also have the potential to take the jobs of the people who performed those functions previously. This is often less skilled workers, who may find it difficult to get employment elsewhere. The primary issue, though, is one of safety. Robots used in medicine must be carefully regulated, to make sure there is no risk of them harming a patient. Regulators are reluctant to allow very much autonomy in medical robots for this reason.

Students who want to become doctors and nurses face many long years of training, first in medical school and then in the hospital. This process is essential to teach them to be qualified, skillful practitioners, with all the medical knowledge and expertise at dealing with patients that they need. Training medical students is also a very expensive process. Over many years, students must be shown what to do by qualified experts, who could otherwise be attending to their own patients.

Other medical skills are learned through practicing them over and over. For example, internally examining a patient or taking a blood sample can be practiced using "dummy" robots. Surgeons also need to practice their surgeries many times before they are safe to perform them alone. They are supervised by qualified surgeons, which is very time-consuming. Using robots can reduce the time and cost of surgical training. Do you think the role of the teacher is at risk here?

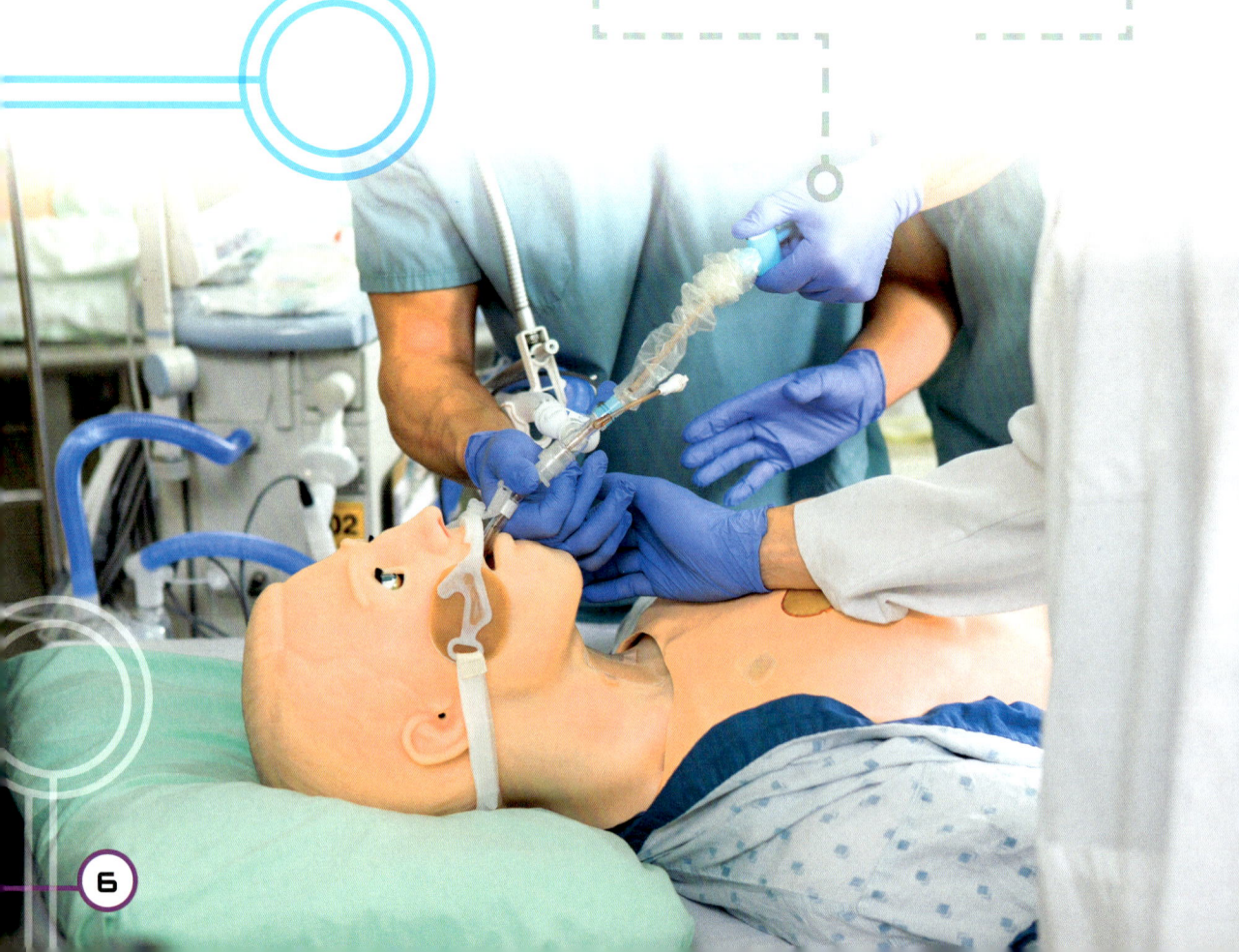

Real-Life Simulation

Although there may be no substitute for the valuable experience of learning about medicine from an expert teacher, or spending time working with real patients, there are some skills that may be taught with the help of robotics. In an emergency room, doctors must quickly decide what is wrong with the patient and how to treat them. Android robots are helping students learn how best to do this. This lifelike robot can describe its symptoms, give blood, and cry out when in pain. It also responds to treatment, showing the students if they are making the right decisions. All these training exercises can be filmed, which makes it easy to give students evaluation of their work.

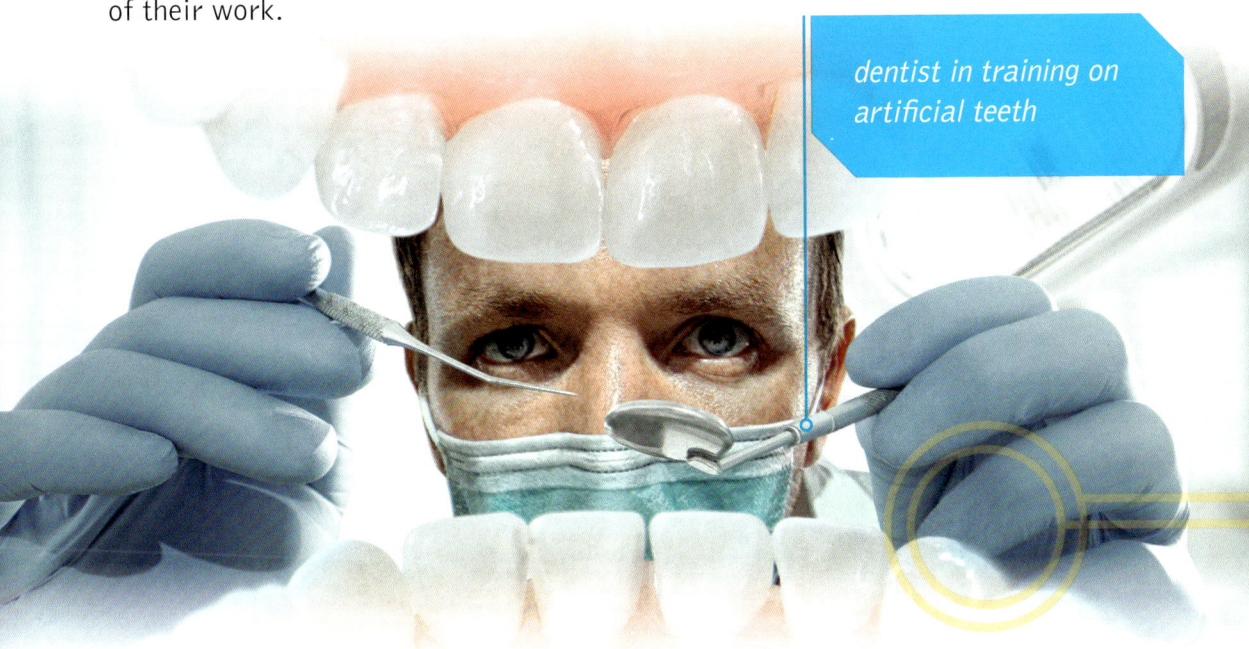

dentist in training on artificial teeth

ROBOT REVOLUTION

Dentists need long, careful training, just the same as doctors. Modern dentistry often involves complex procedures to replace damaged or unsightly teeth. It is not safe for trainees to work on real patients' mouths until they have perfected their skills. Now realistic android robots are being used for this training. Simroid, created in Japan, looks just like a person, and can talk, blink, and move its head. Its teeth are fitted with sensors, and it will cry out in pain if the equipment touches its virtual nerves. Working with these lifelike robots helps to teach the trainees not just to perform the dentistry correctly, but also to interact with their patient as a person.

One of the biggest problems facing medicine today is that many patients pick up an infection while they are being treated in the hospital. This is because there are always infections present, and existing cleaning methods are not entirely effective. This is not what people want when they are already sick, and it can have serious consequences. In 2011, 1 in every 25 patients got an infection during treatment at a healthcare facility in the United States. Even worse, one in nine of those patients died, often because the infections cannot be treated with antibiotics. Because of this, hospitals are looking very closely at their infection-control programs. Traditionally these require a lot of human labor. Part of their plan includes using robots.

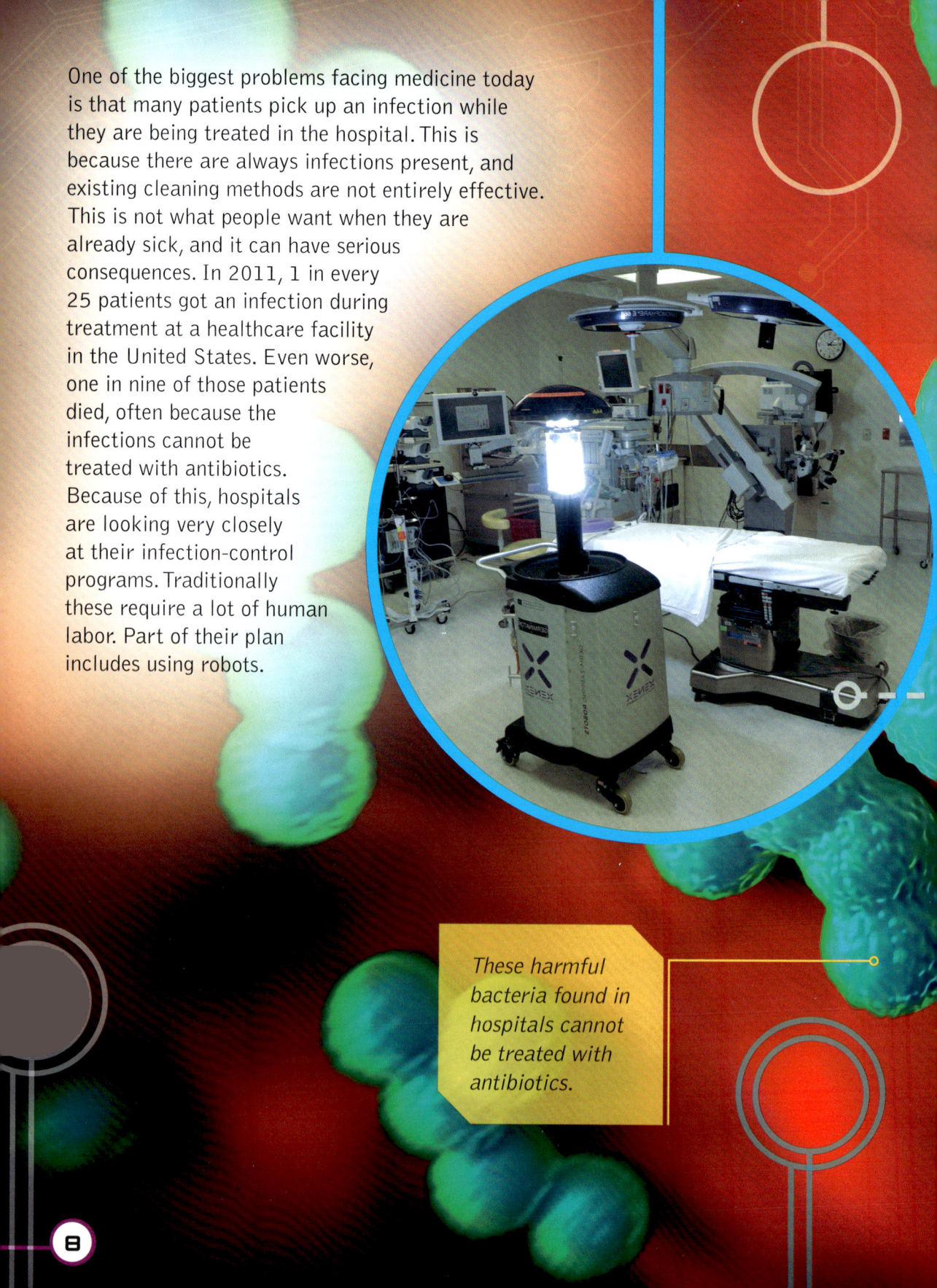

These harmful bacteria found in hospitals cannot be treated with antibiotics.

How Do They Work?

There are two systems available for disinfecting an area using a robot. Both of them kill the bacteria present in the room. The first uses a chemical called hydrogen peroxide. The robot disperses a vapor containing the chemical. This kills the bacteria on contact. This system is effective, but it can take up to three hours to clean a room, and all air vents must be closed as the vapor is dangerous. The second system, which is becoming more popular, uses ultraviolet (UV) light to kill the bacteria. The robot is fitted with large lamps that shine UV light around the room. This can clean a room in 15 minutes, and the robot is left unattended. These robots are being used to clean the most sensitive areas in hospitals, such as operating rooms and intensive care units, where infection can cause the most harm. It uses no chemicals, which is also better for the environment.

> The UV light robots are quicker than the hydrogen peroxide robots. However, it is about twice the price, at around $80,000 each. It also only kills bacteria on the surfaces that the light touches. It may not clean the undersides of objects. So far there is little data on how much of a difference they are making in reducing infection rates, so more time is needed. Can these robots replace humans in this task, or is it only a useful addition to existing, proven hygiene practices, such as handwashing and staff education? What do you think? Give reasons for your answers.

ROBOT REVOLUTION
UV light kills bacteria by attacking the DNA in their cells, making it impossible for them to reproduce or carry out essential life functions.

CHAPTER 2
SURGERY

When a patient has surgery, the surgeon opens up their body to repair or replace the part that is damaged or faulty. This is high-risk medicine, and surgeons train for many years to become expert at their craft. It may seem strange that a robot could help with this highly skilled work. However, combining a surgeon's intelligence and skill with a robot's accuracy and precision is giving some amazing results. Robotics in surgery is a really exciting area of development.

Less Impact

In the past, surgeons would make a large incision to access the problem area of the patient's body. Then the development of "keyhole surgery" made it possible to do many surgeries with smaller incisions. Now, surgeons are getting extra help from robotic systems that allow them to carry out precise procedures through even smaller openings. This creates less scarring for the patient, and generally means it takes less time for them to recover from their surgery.

In conventional eye surgery, like this, the surgeon makes very small, precise movements with the instruments.

Even the most experienced surgeon can have a slightly shaky hand. This can be a problem in extremely precise surgery on small areas, known as microsurgery. One example of this is microsurgery on the eye. This highly sensitive area demands absolute precision in the use of the surgical instruments. Johns Hopkins University developed the Steady-Hand Eye Robot to assist surgeons performing microsurgical procedures in the eye. The surgeon and the robotic manipulator share control of the instrument being used. The surgeon's hand movements control the movements of the robot, but any shake in the surgeon's hand is removed.

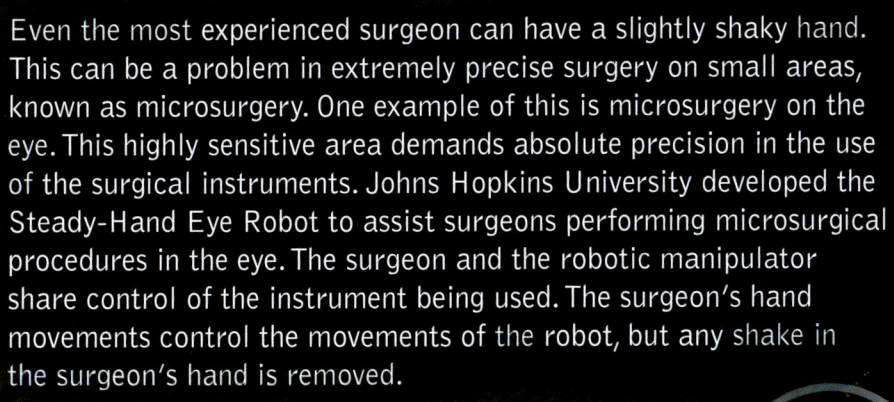

Having surgery is stressful for patients. They like to know that the surgeons have had a lot of experience at performing the procedures, and have a good record of successful outcomes for their patients. Introducing robots to the operating room may cause patients to worry more. Will they be operated on by a machine? Could it go out of control? What happens if something goes wrong? The regulatory authorities are making sure that these worries are addressed before they give approval for any robot in surgery. Why do you think the input of the human surgeon is vitally important?

The first area of surgery to be aided by robots was surgeries involving bones. Although all surgery is difficult, surgery on bones involves working with parts of the body that do not move when they are touched. Several robots have been developed to help with different kinds of orthopedic surgery.

Spinal Surgery

Operating on the spine is difficult. The bones in the spine, called vertebrae, are hard and fixed. Vertebrae are surrounded by bundles of nerves and if these are damaged, the patient can lose the use of parts of their body. It is vitally important, therefore, to be precise when operating to target exactly the right spot. The Renaissance robot can help with this. Before the surgery, the software in the robot uses three-dimensional (3D) scans to analyze the patient's anatomy, vertebra by vertebra, helping the surgeon to plan ahead and design the ideal procedure for each patient.

The Renaissance robot is not much bigger than a soda can. During surgery, it is directly anchored to the spine of the patient. It can bend and rotate, to place its arm on the spine in a specific location and help the surgeon to place implants through small incisions in the body. The surgeon's skill is still needed to use this tool effectively.

Then, during surgery, a guidance unit on the robot can position the surgeon's instruments exactly, allowing for 0.06 inch (1.5 mm) accuracy. This is important because it reduces the damage to surrounding tissue, resulting in less bleeding, smaller scars, less pain, and faster recovery.

Another orthopedic surgery robot is TSolution One. This robot is excellent at delivering precise cutting of bones, so it is used in surgeries such as hip joint replacements. It too uses scans to help the surgeon tailor the surgery exactly to the patient. Then it creates precise, clean cuts in the existing bones so that the new artificial joints can be inserted in exactly the right place.

ROBOT REVOLUTION

Scoliosis is an abnormal curvature of the spine that affects approximately 7 million people in the United States. Severe cases are treated by corrective surgery, where devices are implanted to help straighten the spine. Robot-guided surgery has been successful in doing this. In a study of 120 teenagers with scoliosis, robot-guided surgery was 99.7 percent accurate in positioning 1,815 implants.

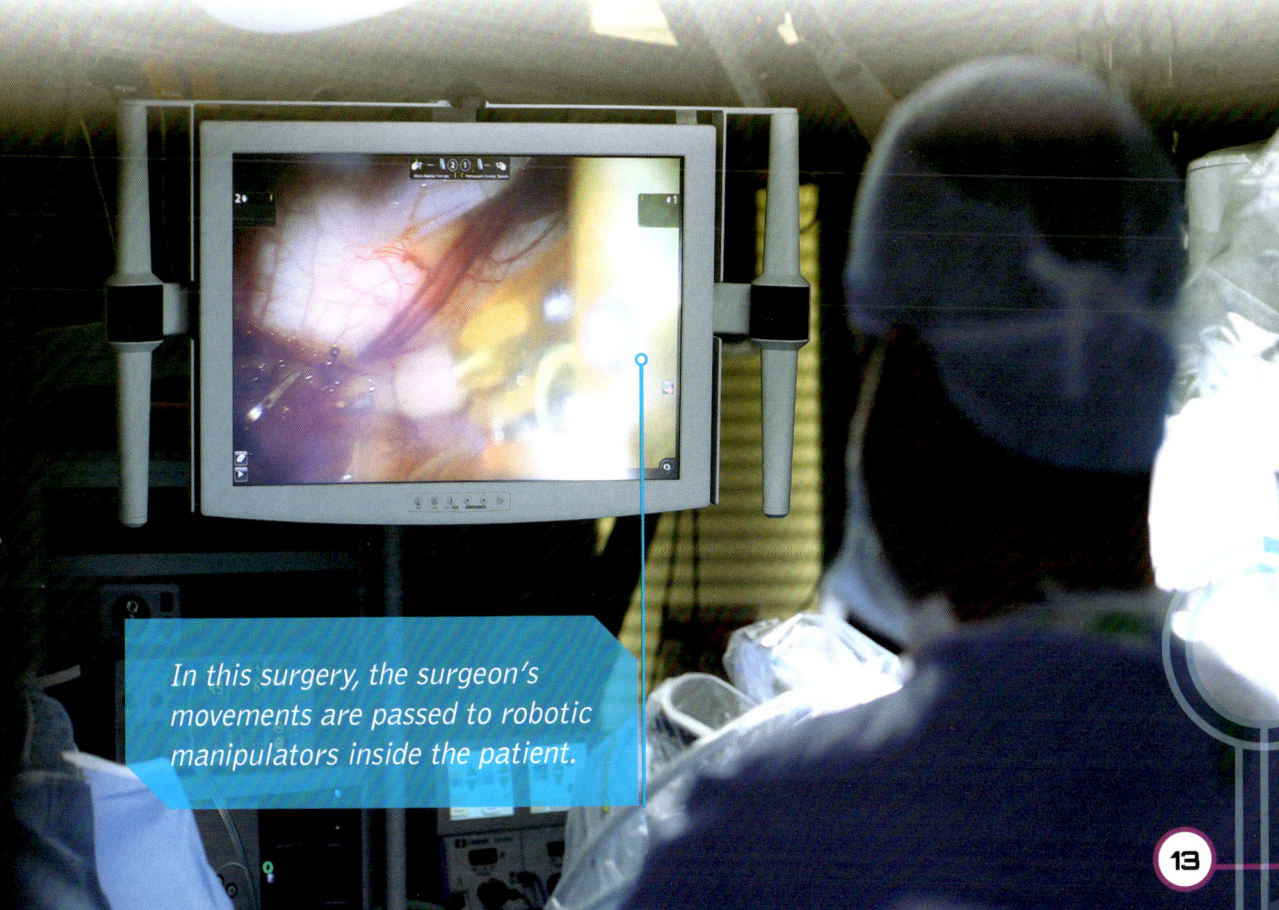

In this surgery, the surgeon's movements are passed to robotic manipulators inside the patient.

Surgical procedures on bones involve working on hard, fixed targets. Surgery on soft tissue, such as the heart or stomach, is much more messy and more difficult to control. The soft tissue moves when it is touched, and it is easily damaged with surgical instruments. Even in this most delicate area of surgery, however, robots have been playing a vital role for several years.

The da Vinci System

The state-of-the-art robot for soft tissue surgery is the da Vinci system. This incredible machine has four arms, and each one has a greater range of movement than a human hand. It is a large machine, almost filling a standard sized operating room. Of course it is not able to operate autonomously. The surgeon sits at a console and manipulates the controls of all four arms. The movements of the controls are then translated into precise movements by the instruments on the ends of the arms.

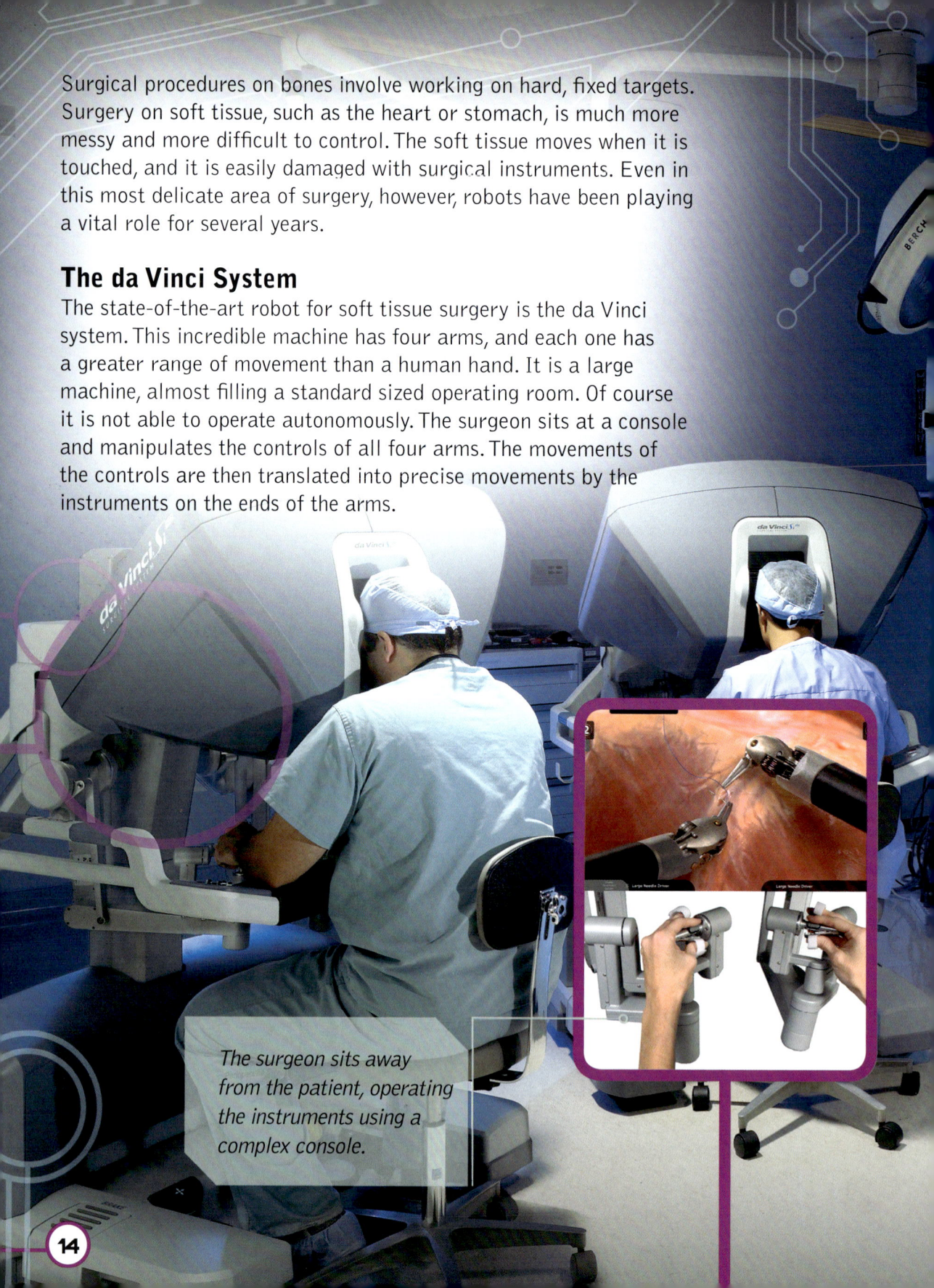

The surgeon sits away from the patient, operating the instruments using a complex console.

Using such a powerful surgical tool raises an important question. Is it safe? A few years after the first versions of the da Vinci system were introduced in the early 2000s, questions were raised about its safety after some patients complained of complications following their surgery. An official investigation was launched. The maker of the system said that later models have addressed any safety issues, and that it is extremely important for surgeons to be fully trained in using it properly. If they are, they say, the da Vinci system is no more risky than regular surgery. Would you risk it?

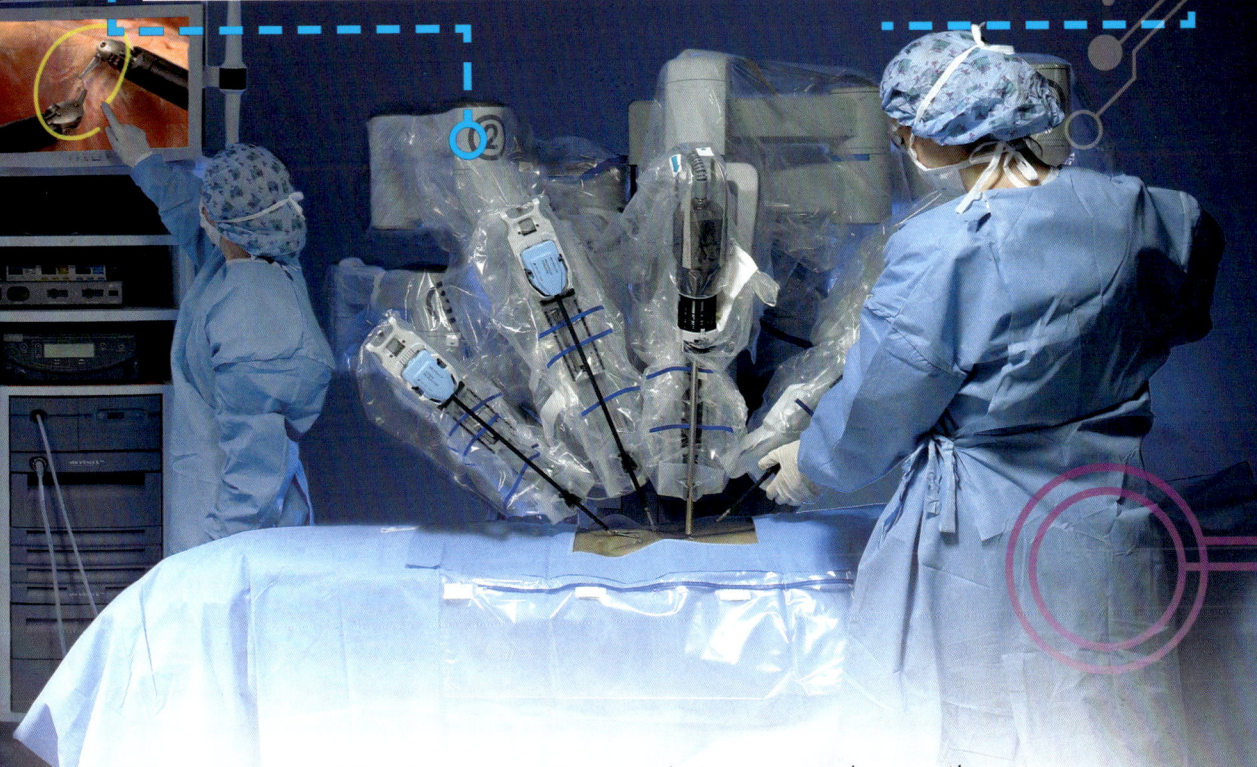

The system magnifies the view of the area being operated on, so the surgeon can see in greater detail than they would be able to with just their eyes. This allows them to perform smaller, more precise movements on the patient's body, using the robot's small instruments. Another important advantage of operating using the da Vinci system is that the incisions in the body can be smaller, too. This causes less damage to the patient, so they can recover more quickly. Surgeons have noticed that patients have been leaving the hospital a few days after surgery, instead of the three to four weeks it would have taken in the past.

The da Vinci system is very expensive. Each one costs about $2 million, and has high maintenance costs too, such as replacing the instruments regularly. Does it make enough of a difference to patients' outcomes to justify this high cost? It can be tough for hospitals to justify spending that kind of money. Do you think it is worth it?

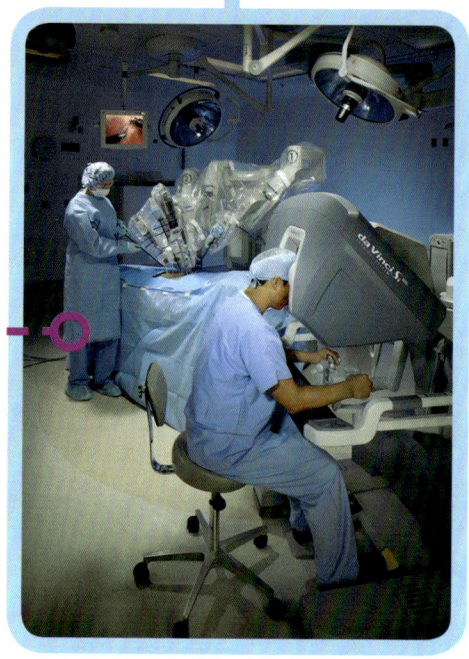

The da Vinci system has been adopted by thousands of hospitals in the United States since it was first introduced in 2000. It has been used to perform millions of surgeries, and many patients have been successfully treated.

Benefit to Patients and Surgeons

Many of the surgeries have been to remove cancerous tumors, especially in parts of the body where making a large incision could cause significant damage. Cancer is one of the biggest killers in the western world, and physicians are looking at all possible ways to increase the number of patients who survive a cancer diagnosis. This robotic equipment has a role to play in the fight against cancer. It is also being used in the fight against another big killer, heart disease. The small instruments can repair faulty areas of the heart. This could mean patients will not need a heart transplant, which is a much more major surgery.

Surgeons, too, can benefit from the da Vinci system. Performing surgery is physically demanding. In regular surgery, the surgeon must stand beside the patient, sometimes for several hours. In keyhole surgery, they must look up repeatedly from the patient to a monitor, where the site of the surgery is shown magnified in size. All this puts a strain on the surgeon's neck, shoulders, and back. Using this robotic system, however, the surgeon sits at a console to operate the instruments remotely. This is much less tiring, and it is therefore possible to perform more surgeries, more quickly, and more successfully.

ROBOT REVOLUTION

Another area of controversy with the da Vinci system is the amount of training that surgeons need to use it effectively. It is a complex piece of equipment. Surgeons have been trained to work directly on the body, developing great expertise on how human anatomy works and a "feel" for their delicate work. Can they perform as well when they are sitting across the room from their patient, looking at the site of the surgery on a screen and controlling instruments that are not in their hands? Surgeons say it takes around 35 to 40 training cases to get used to using the robotics, but after that it feels like an extension of their own arms.

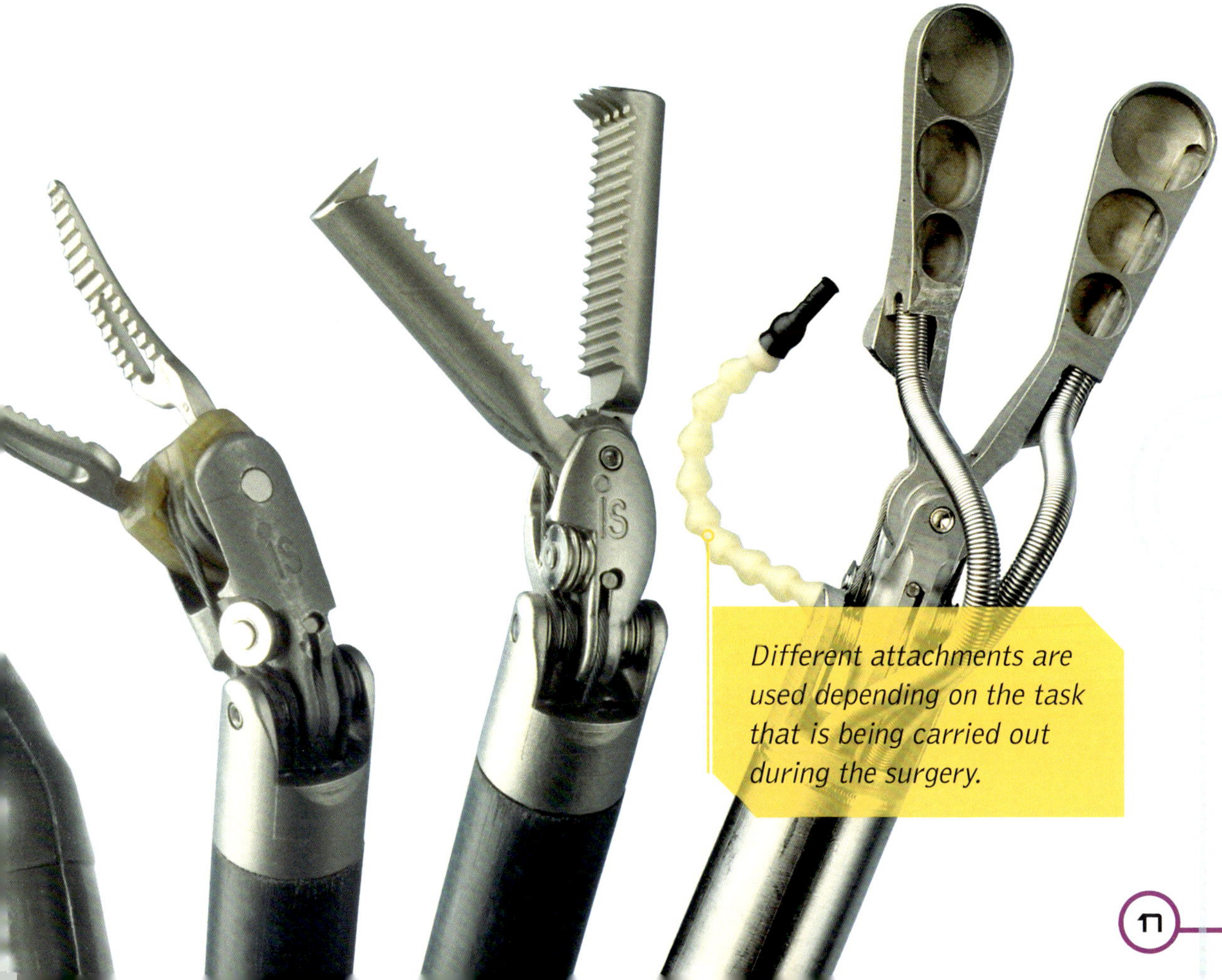

Different attachments are used depending on the task that is being carried out during the surgery.

Surgery is often needed to repair a damaged part of the body. This may be an internal organ, such as the intestines, or a deep cut from the outside, for example if an arm or leg is badly broken in an accident. An important part of these surgeries is the surgeon's ability to sew up the repaired tissue effectively. This highly skilled work, called suturing, takes a lot of training and experience. Researchers have been trying to see if a robotic machine could be capable of performing this challenging work.

STAR

The robot they have devised is called the Smart Tissue Autonomous Robot (STAR). In 2016, this bot was tested in a trial to stitch together the intestines of a pig that had been cut through. It was rather like repairing a garden hose, so that water would not leak out of it after its repair.

STAR uses 3D cameras to keep focus on its target, and adjusts its movements as the tissues move during the procedure. However, many surgeons would be concerned about the safety of letting a robot perform this delicate work inside a patient. Do you think that a robot like this can replace a surgeon? What risks do you think are involved in robots doing work like this?

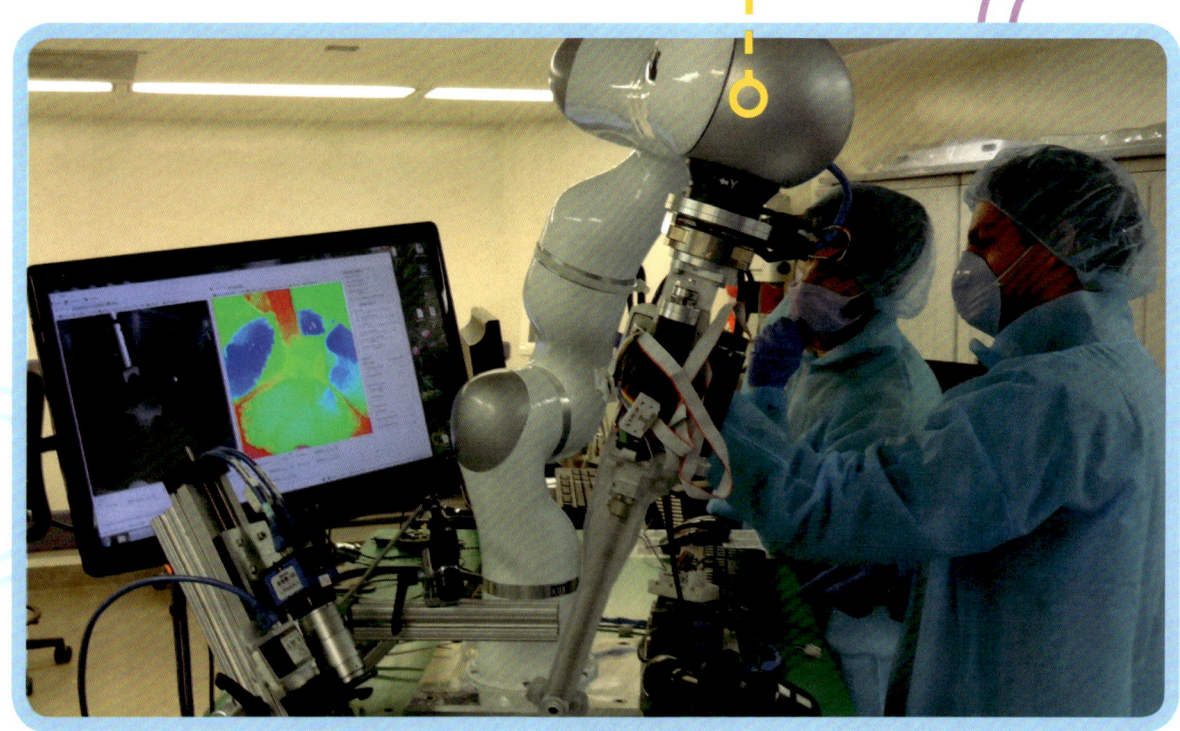

STAR used its own vision, tools, and intelligence to carry out the procedure. Surgeons performed the same suturing exercise at the same time. The remarkable result was that the robot did a better job of the suturing than the human surgeons. Its stitches were more regular, and they were more resistant to leaking. This does not mean, though, that robots are likely to take over this process in operating rooms any time soon. First, STAR was programmed by humans, with information from the best techniques used by surgeons.

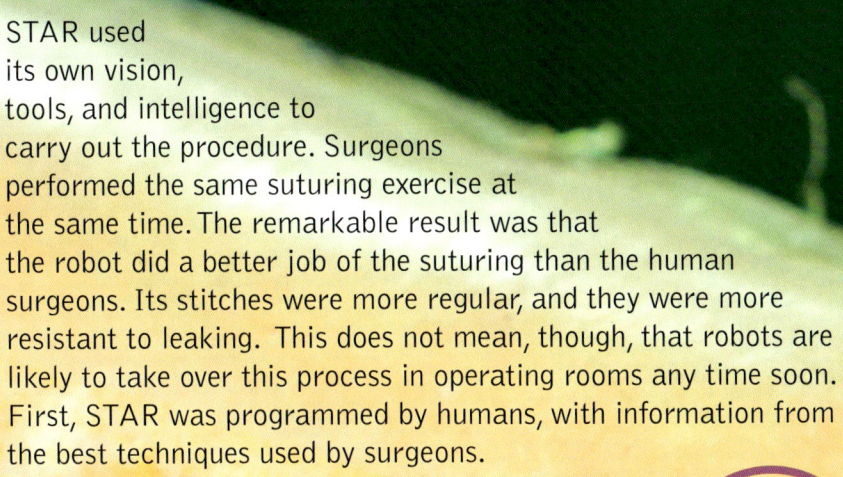

Surgical wounds are sewn up. The threads are removed or dissolved once the wound has healed.

Second, even during the trial, STAR did receive some human help. In about 40 percent of the procedures a human hand intervened, for example, to hold a thread.

STAR showed that a robot can perform soft tissue surgery successfully, but it is not necessary. A robot may be quick and accurate, but surgeons are already skilled at this work. Additionally, in many instances suturing is done not with thread but with staples. These do the job of sealing the tissues in a matter of seconds. Perhaps the cost of this expensive technology cannot yet be justified by the benefit it brings to medicine.

Some areas of the body are difficult for surgeons to access, such as the brain, the throat, and the lungs. The brain is obviously very sensitive, and damaging it can cause serious harm to the patient, or even death. The throat and neck are difficult because it is physically awkward to reach them with surgical equipment. One new kind of robot has been developed to help solve this problem, and it is expanding the reach of surgery.

A Flexible Robot

Flex® is a flexible, bio-inspired snake-like robot that allows surgeons to perform minimally invasive surgery on parts of the throat that are hard to reach. This tube-like equipment is inserted into the patient's mouth and carefully guided down the throat by the surgeon, using a joystick.

The path that Flex® takes must be decided by a surgeon; the robot is not autonomous at that point. However, once the procedure at the site is completed, it becomes autonomous. It can steer itself back up and out of the patient's body, because it "learned" the correct route on the way in. The authorities that regulate the development of surgical robots are concerned to be sure no robot can take control of a procedure, because they fear it could harm patients. Do you think surgery will always require the skill of a surgeon? Can you imagine that one day a robot could be programmed to perform the whole surgery autonomously? Should this be allowed to happen? Give reasons for your answers.

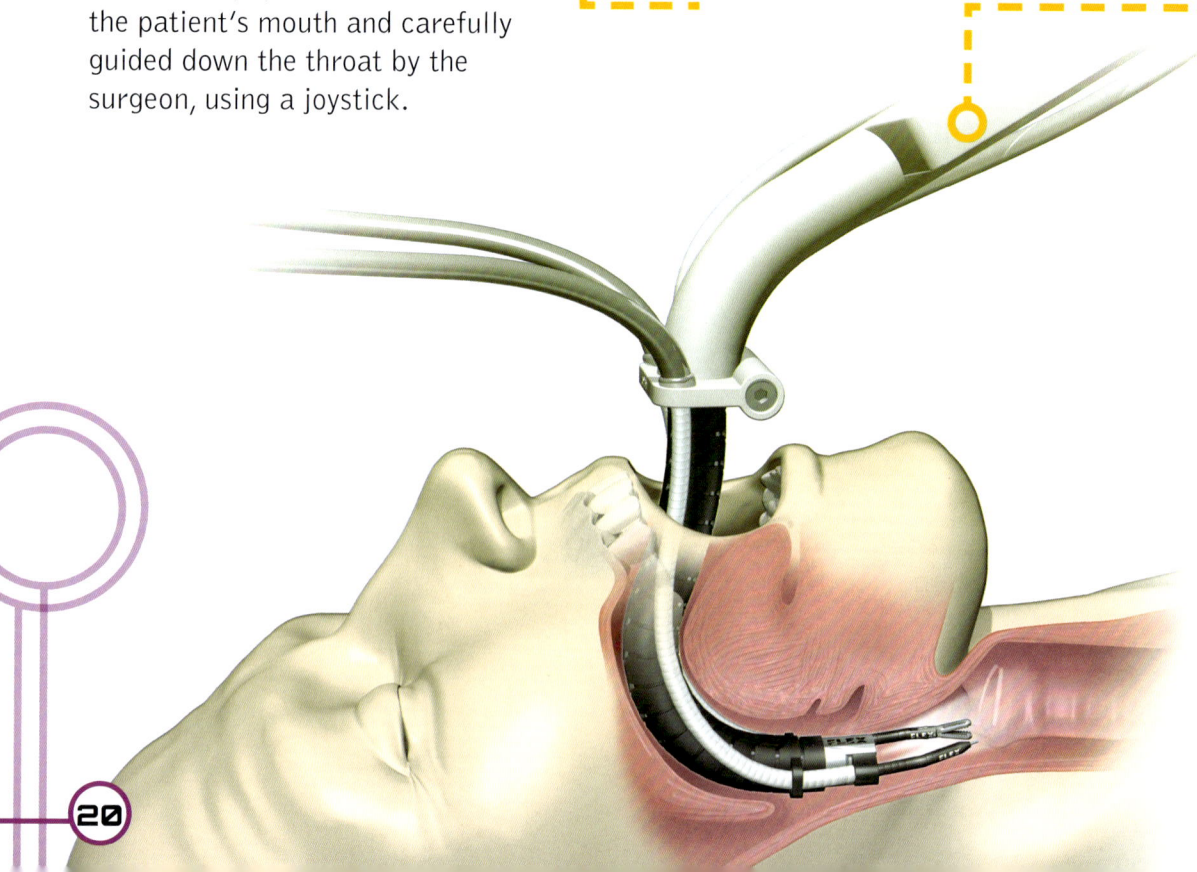

Flex® is pioneering surgery on areas of the body that are difficult to reach with traditional surgical techniques.

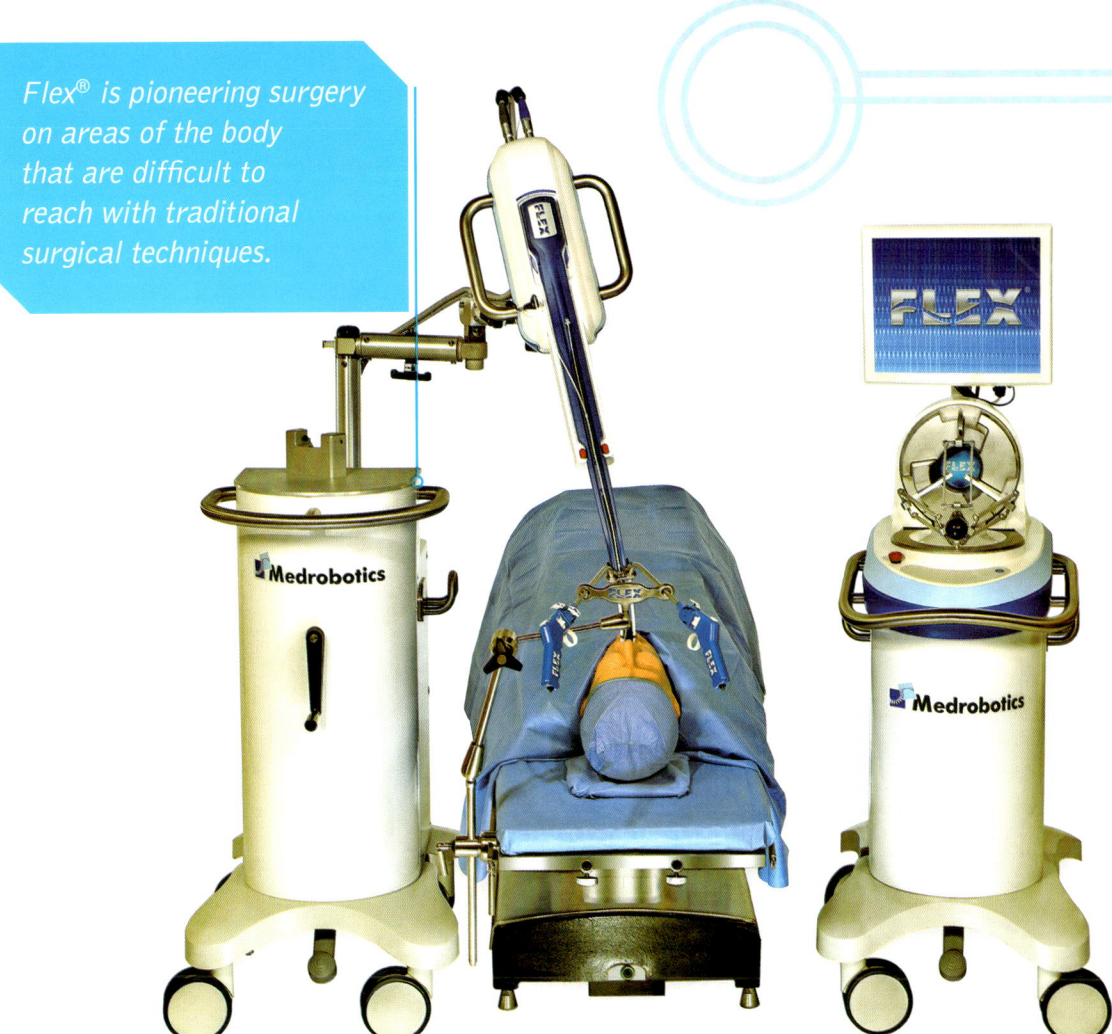

A camera on the end of Flex® shows the surgeon what is inside, as it twists and turns through the patient's airway. In the past, to reach these regions surgeons had to break the patient's jaw to open their mouth wide enough, or make a large incision in the neck. Both of these had an impact on the patient's ability to recover fully and in a short time.

ROBOT REVOLUTION

Once Flex® reaches the site to be operated on, it stiffens to create a stable platform for the surgical instruments. These are then inserted through two smaller tubes on the sides of the main one, and controlled by the surgeon. The surgeon has a kit of tools to use, such as scalpels, scissors, grippers, and a needle. They can cut out a tumor, for example, or sew up an internal wound.

One area of medicine that has become increasingly popular in recent years is cosmetic surgery. As people get older, more people are turning to surgeons to try to keep them looking young. Facelifts, tucks, and injections are all designed to reverse the natural process where skin ages and sags as it becomes less elastic. For some people, especially men, the most pressing problem of aging is hair loss. This generally begins at the front of the head, and the hairline gradually recedes over the years. Robots can help to restore this condition.

Surgeons have been performing hair transplants for many years. Decades ago, a long strip of the scalp would be removed from the back of the head, where hairs were plentiful. The hairs would then be removed and inserted in the bald patch, one by one, by the surgeon. This painful surgery left a scar and recovery times were long. More recently, surgeons have harvested individual hairs one at a time, using a motorized tool. This requires precise, monotonous movements thousands of times for a single procedure. It is exhausting for the surgeon, requiring a high level of eye-hand coordination and manual dexterity.

ARTAS™ scans the head for the best hairs to harvest and transplant.

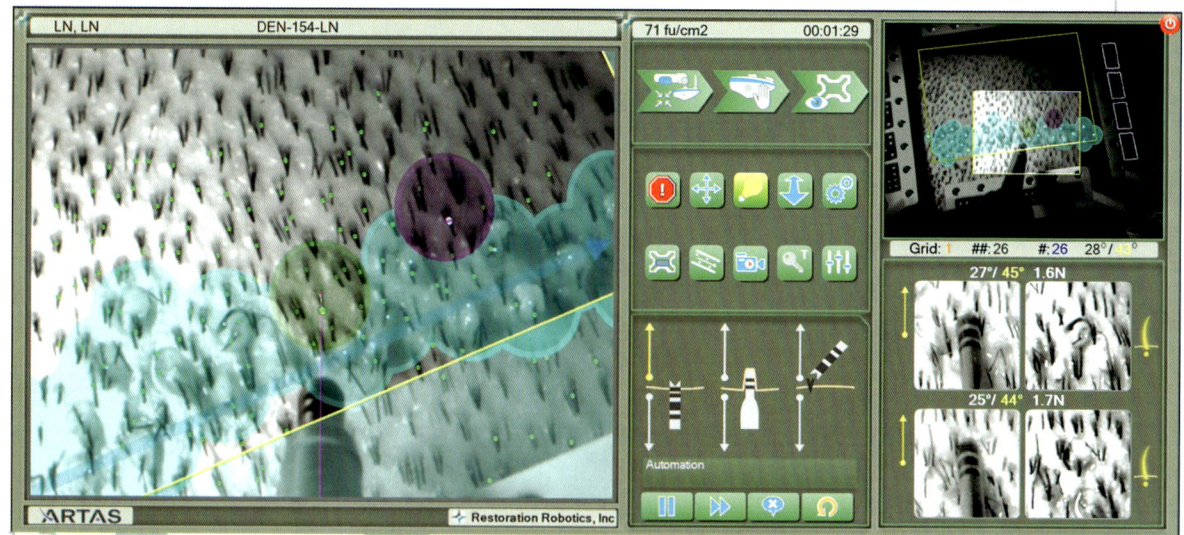

Robotic Hair Restoration

A new robot called ARTAS™ can assist in hair restoration, with the guidance of a surgeon. Each hair is targeted individually with robotic precision. No stitches are needed. It identifies the healthiest hairs on the back of the head for harvesting, then removes the whole follicle. Once the hair follicles are harvested, the ARTAS™ System precisely creates new donor sites. Using artificial intelligence algorithms, existing permanent hair is protected while creating a natural result.

The advantages of the ARTAS™ System are obvious. It is a much less invasive procedure than the strip surgery. It also improves on the surgeon's individual hair restoration. It is less painful, quicker, more accurate, and does not cause fatigue in the surgeon, which can lead to errors. However, it is more expensive than traditional procedures.

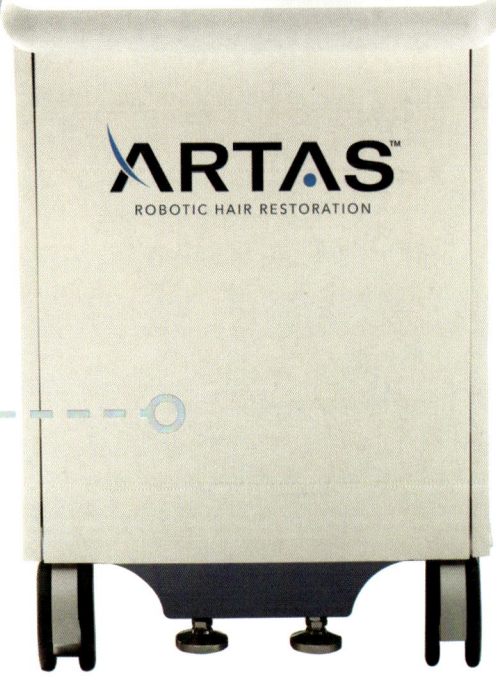

ARTAS™ analyzes, tracks, and monitors each hair 60 times per second. It can even detect the healthy hairs in the thinned area of the head receiving new hairs, and avoid damaging them during site making and implantation. The surgeon is still needed, however. They design the area to be transplanted, and control the angle and direction at which the new hairs are inserted, so they grow in the most natural-looking way. Perhaps this is an example of what robots can do best—a monotonous and potentially dangerous task. What do you think?

CHAPTER 3
REHABILITATION AND MOBILITY

One of the most important areas of healthcare is getting people back on their feet after they have been sick. They may have had surgery, or an accident, or an illness that has kept them in bed for a long period. This work is known as rehabilitation, or rehab for short. It can be slow work, and it takes expert care. Even here, however, there is a role for robotic technology to play.

Powerful Aides

Over the past few years, some patients who were told they were unlikely ever to walk again have been given new hope by a powerful robotic exoskeleton. This is basically a pair of powered robotic legs that the patient wears. They place their feet on the plates then secure straps around their legs, hips, and trunk. A computer in a backpack can power the robotic components for hours, providing powered hip and knee motion. This helps the wearer stand, walk, and even climb stairs. A therapist oversees the robot's use. They can change the amount of power given to each leg, depending on how much the patient can do unaided. They know how to do this because the software in the robot collects data from sensors in the exoskeleton to figure out how much power is needed.

At the moment these machines are very expensive. They are mostly being used in hospitals and rehabilitation clinics around the world, where they are helping many people improve their mobility. These people, however, want to be able to get around on their own feet back home, and out in the community. Robotic exoskeletons are now beginning to be cleared for this kind of personal use as well. This can give people back their freedom, allowing them to go back to work and live a normal life without the constant help or supervision of caregivers.

These robotic exoskeletons are powerful machines and they operate with a high degree of autonomy. This is especially true of the versions that people use at home, instead of in a clinical setting. How do you think they should be regulated, to make sure they are safe for individuals to use?

ROBOT REVOLUTION

The exoskeleton transfers the wearer's weight to the ground, and she uses two arm braces to keep herself from falling over. Walking is a collaborative process: when the wearer shifts her weight to the left, she triggers the robotic leg on the right to take a step forward. Then she shifts her weight to the right for the next step, resulting in a slow but surprisingly natural movement.

When a patient has suffered a major injury to their body, they need help to get moving again. They may have been in an accident, or had a stroke, and their ability to use their limbs is impaired. The experts who give mobility care to these patients are physiotherapists. They give patients physiotherapy, in the form of exercises and other treatments to build their muscle strength and get them moving again.

Physiotherapy is very labor-intensive. One or more physiotherapists work with the patient for up to one hour at a time, generally several times a day. It is important for the patients' recovery for the exercises to be done regularly if they are to regain muscle strength. They must build on their progress each day. It is also important that the exercises are tailored exactly to the needs of the patient. They must address the precise mobility problem they have, create progress, but not push the patient too far, which could cause more harm.

Robotic systems are now being developed to help with physiotherapy. One system is the intelligent pneumatic arm movement (iPAM) robot. This robot delivers arm exercises to people who have suffered a stroke. It consists of two powered robotic arms that copy the way a physiotherapist helps the patient. It holds their arm in two places and coordinates the joints to make the arm move in normal patterns. One advantage of these robots is they can deliver intense physiotherapy, for a longer time, with only indirect supervision from the physiotherapist. This frees the experts to deliver treatment to more patients.

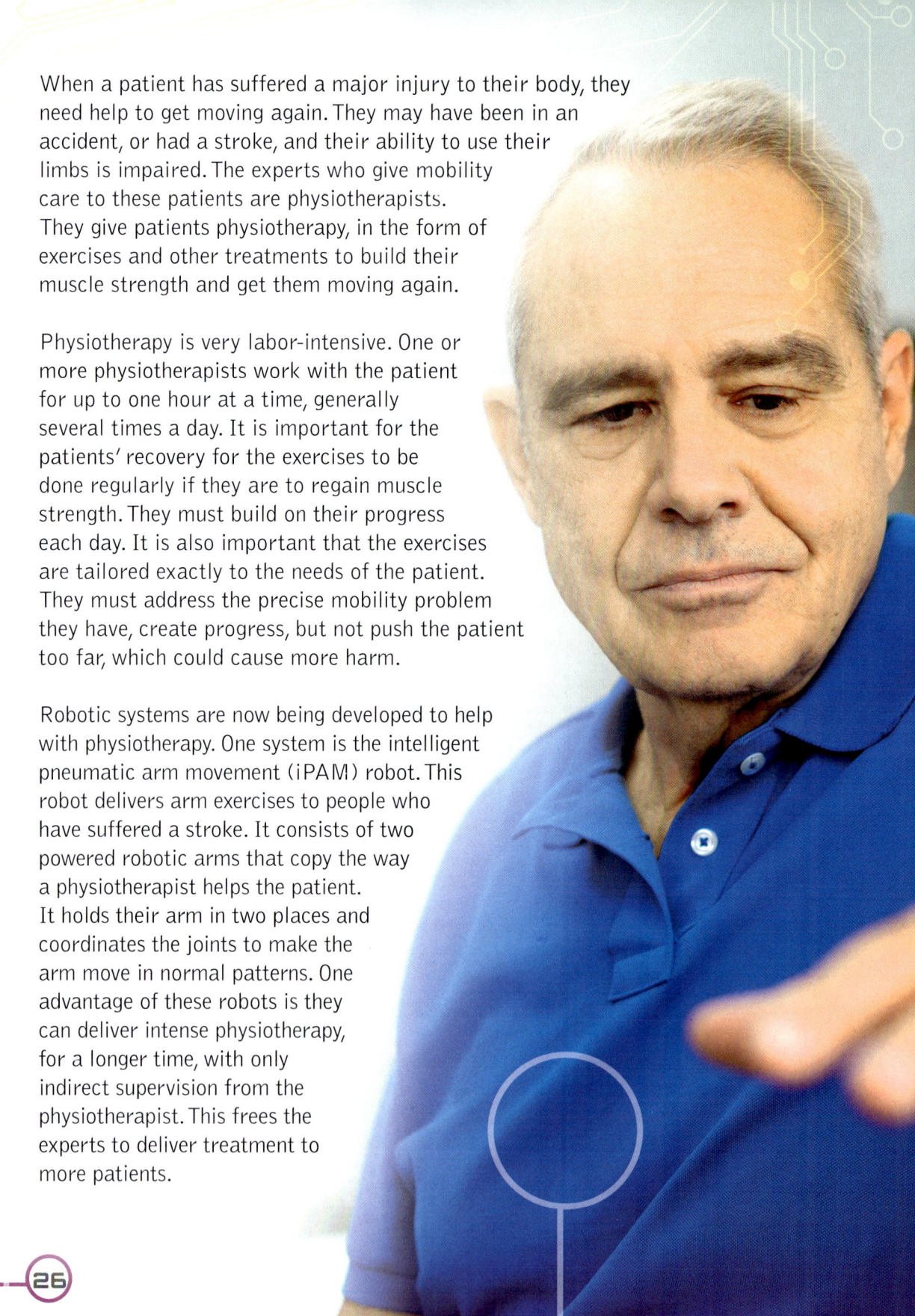

To develop successful robotic systems to do the work of human physiotherapists, a combination of high quality mechanical and electrical design with innovative software engineering is needed. The designers engage with both patients and therapists in the design process to get them just right. Safety is critical, as these powerful systems are connected directly to human users. Do you think it is right that they can operate autonomously? How should they be regulated?

Playing Games

Another robot-assisted rehabilitation method takes the form of a powered arm support worn by the patient, who then uses it to play simple games on a computer screen. The robot "reads" what the patient can and cannot do, and learns how and when to encourage movement. This gradual approach encourages muscle and nerve connections to regrow. The robot also collects data in its computer of how well the patient has done, so their progress can be measured.

Physiotherapy strengthens the muscles, which are made up of fibers. The muscles move when the brain sends signals along nerves, or neurons, to the fibers.

CHAPTER 4

NURSING AND WELL-BEING

Healthcare providers around the world face big challenges in finding enough qualified staff to meet the needs of the growing and aging population. As people live longer, their medical needs often increase and become more complex. The strain this places on medical services is huge. People are looking to robotics to try to ease some of this pressure. A key area under investigation is one where face-to-face contact has always seemed to be essential, and that is nursing. Perhaps robots can help with nurses' exhausting and heavy workload.

Heavy Lifting

The physical strain of taking care of a patient in bed can be considerable. Many nurses suffer from bad backs, painful legs, and other complaints. For many years there have been mechanical aides for lifting patients in bed, and transferring them from one place to another. However, these are often bulky and awkward. Now, technology has created a robot that can help nurses with this task. It is called the Hybrid Assistive Limb (HAL) system. HAL for Care Support (Lumbar Type) is an artificially-powered device that users wear around their lumbar region, which is around the lower back and hips. It gives them extra, powered support in this region, reduces the stress on the body, and enables them to lift heavy loads.

HAL for Care Support is powered by a battery, which means it can be easily carried and used in a variety of locations, such as a hospital ward, a care home bedroom, or a patient's own home. It is also light, so the caregiver can wear it for several hours at a time. The main issue with aides like these is their high cost. How many people will be able to afford to take advantage of the benefits they offer?

This can make a big difference to the care of elderly and disabled patients. Experienced nurses are able to work for longer. They are less likely to have to stop work because of back injuries. The patient benefits, too, knowing they are being moved safely.

Looking after patients in bed puts a big physical strain on nursing staff.

ROBOT REVOLUTION

HAL for Care Support can assist the wearer to move exactly as they want. Brain signals sent to the muscles telling them to move are picked up by the sensors on HAL. They then tell the robot how to move in exactly the best way to support the caregiver as they lift the patient.

Sometimes a nurse, or even several nurses, cannot lift a patient, even with the help of a robotic aid like HAL for Care Support. In these situations, they need more heavyweight help. Fortunately, robot developers in Japan have been working on this problem, too, and have come up with some incredible solutions.

Robear is an android nursing robot, designed to lift and mobilize elderly or infirm patients in hospitals or care homes. Robear is shaped like a bear. It has a friendly face and ears, and can bend at the waist as it lifts a weight of up to 175 lb (80 kg) in its large, padded arms. It can lift a patient from a wheelchair to a bed, for example, or help them stand up.

Robear is designed to replace rather than assist nurses and other health professionals. Some people worry that the skills of these professionals are under threat because of this technology. Others think that a human's skills and ability to interact with patients will remain essential. Robear is still only a research project for now, as its developers continue to improve its technology and ensure that it can be used with absolute safety.

Terapio

One time-consuming part of the work of nurses is collecting routine health data on their patients and entering it into the hospital's recording systems. Terapio is designed to help with this. This Japanese robot is programmed to follow a nurse on their rounds. There is a touch display panel on the top to input collected data straight into the patient's record. The patient history and medications are available instantly on the robot's display for reference. When not displaying data, the display shows the robot's friendly "face."

The shape of Terapio's eyes change to convey emotion. Using robots to collect data demands computer programs that do not fail, or data could be misplaced or hacked. Do you think this is safer or less safe than relying on people to input the data?

ROBOT REVOLUTION
Robear has sensors that allow its movements to be guided by a nurse, who can also program it to send it to various locations, such as a patient's room. It even has voice-activation, so that a nurse can control it simply by speaking.

Terapio uses its manipulator arm to obtain data on patients' vital signs, such as their temperature.

The population is growing older, as more people are living longer. What every elderly person wants, however, is a good quality of life, whatever their age. This means being in good enough health to be able to live life as they choose. Most people want to live independently in their own home. As they get older this can become more difficult, as they are less able to get around or they find it a challenge to manage everyday tasks. Advances in robotics offer some help to the elderly, to allow them to cope better at home.

Nursebot

Pearl is a Nursebot. This robot is a personal assistant, to help with daily tasks and provide a little companionship. It can recognize the speech of its owner, and follow them around. A touchscreen on the robot can give instructions. For example, it can remind its owner to take their medication, to attend an appointment, or to do their exercises. It is very useful for researching what people would like to have a robot do for them.

Researchers who developed Pearl more than 10 years ago were curious to know how important it was for these robots to look human. They experimented with altering the eyes, mouth, and other facial features, to make them as attractive as possible to their owners. They found that humans want to have an emotional connection with their robots, and its appearance is important for this, but if it looks too lifelike, people find it creepy. There is an ideal balance.

The use of Nursebots could help elderly people to stay active more safely in their own homes.

Robots such as these are still not being widely used, but in the future they could be able to make the difference for an elderly person between being able to live independently and having to move to a nursing home. There is a benefit to medical and social services, too, because their costs are reduced if people can stay at home. As more of the mainstream population uses robots in their homes to perform everyday tasks, the technology used in nursebots should advance rapidly.

In the future, nursebots like this are likely to be able to do even more. They should be able to collect data on the owner's health and report it back to physicians and nurses at a health center or hospital. This kind of telehealth capability would be really useful for elderly patients who find it difficult to leave the house for medical appointments. Can you think of any downsides to the use of a nursebot like Pearl?

Robots are not only useful in medicine for performing mechanical and practical tasks. One very important area of medicine is mental health, when patients do not have a physical illness but they are unwell in their mind. They might be depressed, which involves feelings of sadness and hopelessness, or they may be confused about what is real and unreal. It is normal for mental sharpness to decline as people age, but patients suffering from an illness called dementia gradually lose almost all their mental capacity.

How Robots Help

People are living longer, which is great, but it can bring problems, too, if the elderly are not in good health. Some people may simply feel low because they are lonely. Others may have more serious conditions. In both cases, doctors recognize the importance of giving elderly people some mental stimulation. This is where robotics comes in. Scientists in Japan have developed a robotic furry seal pup called Paro.

Using artificial intelligence, Paro can respond to being stroked or hugged, and to being spoken to. It has soft fur and large eyes, to make it appealing. People interacting with Paro experience a physical and emotional interaction that makes them feel good, even though often they realize they are interacting with a "toy."

The cognitive therapy that robot pets such as Paro provide is not just pleasant for the elderly patients, it is important medically. It can delay the progress of mental health problems, improving the patients' quality of life and cutting medical and social care costs. Robots like Paro can help in these ways. Do you think there is a danger they could be seen as an "easy fix" of problems that require more complex health and social services? Give reasons for your answer.

Staff at nursing homes where Paro has been introduced since 2003 say it has a huge impact on residents. It offers a kind of therapy similar to interacting with pets such as cats and dogs. Unlike real animals, however, Paro does not get bored and wander off, or shed fur, or bite. It also does not need feeding, or risk spreading infection. It is always there for a cuddle when needed.

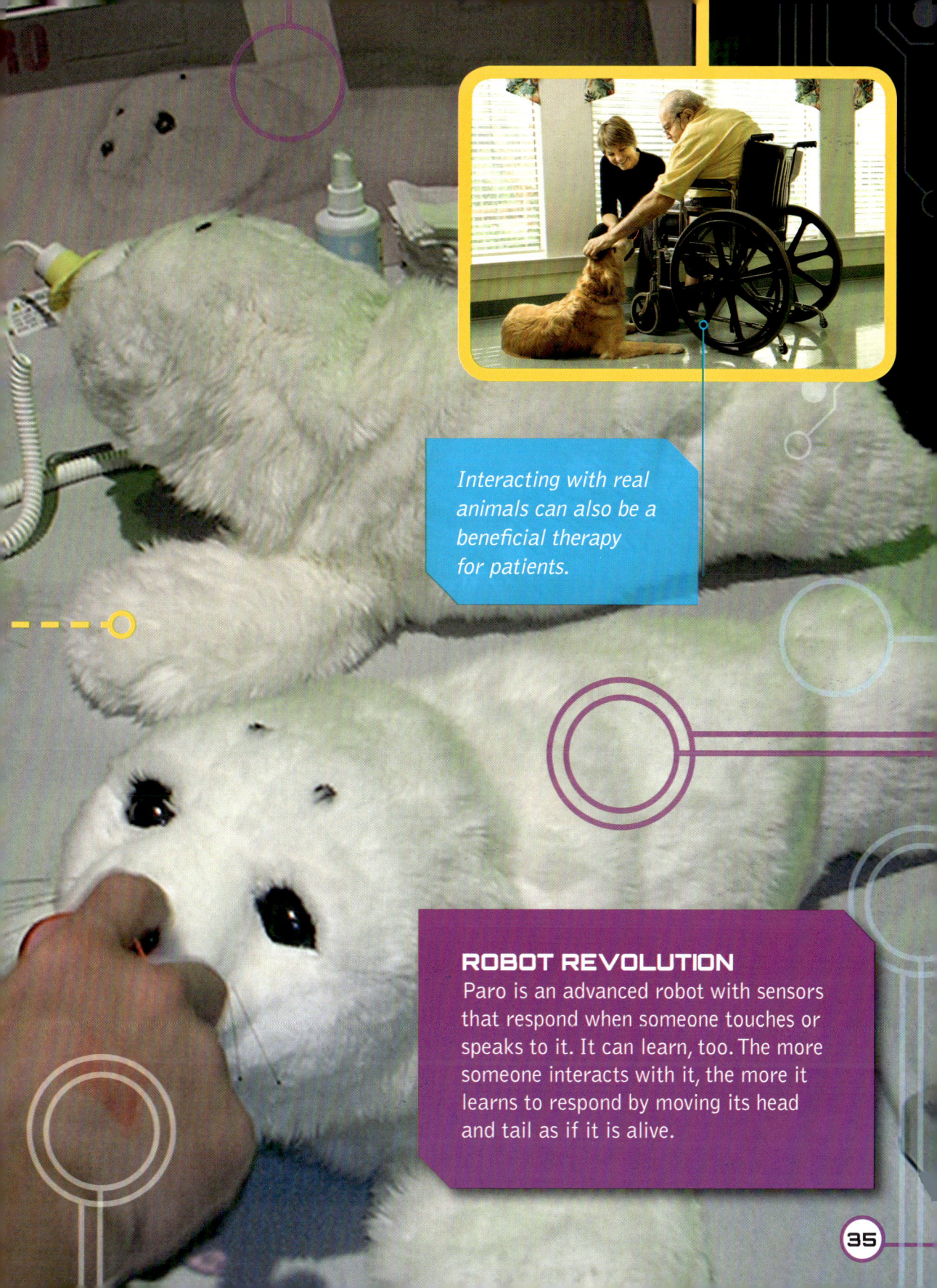

Interacting with real animals can also be a beneficial therapy for patients.

ROBOT REVOLUTION

Paro is an advanced robot with sensors that respond when someone touches or speaks to it. It can learn, too. The more someone interacts with it, the more it learns to respond by moving its head and tail as if it is alive.

CHAPTER 5
DELIVERING DRUGS

Drugs are a vitally important part of the world of modern medicine. Millions of people take prescription medications every day. Some are to help them recover from surgery, some are to prevent conditions they already have from worsening, and some are to protect us from catching diseases. The methods used to deliver these drugs to the body vary, from injections and patches to pills and liquids. Now, researchers are excited at the prospect of using robots to do this important work.

Microbots

For a robot to deliver a drug to a patient's body and travel through the blood vessels it must be very small. These amazing robots are called microbots. The extraordinary thing about them is that they are designed to deliver drugs to a specific location by being controlled remotely. Scientists have studied the way that bacteria move through the body, and have used what they learned to design the shape of the microbots, so that they can move to where they are needed. If a collection of the microbots could deliver a dose of drugs directly to where they were needed, it could reduce the chance of side effects on the rest of the body. It would also target the disease at precise times and in precise locations, using less of the drug than the normal methods. This is a major trend in the development of medicine today, targeting treatments more precisely, for all kinds of medical problems.

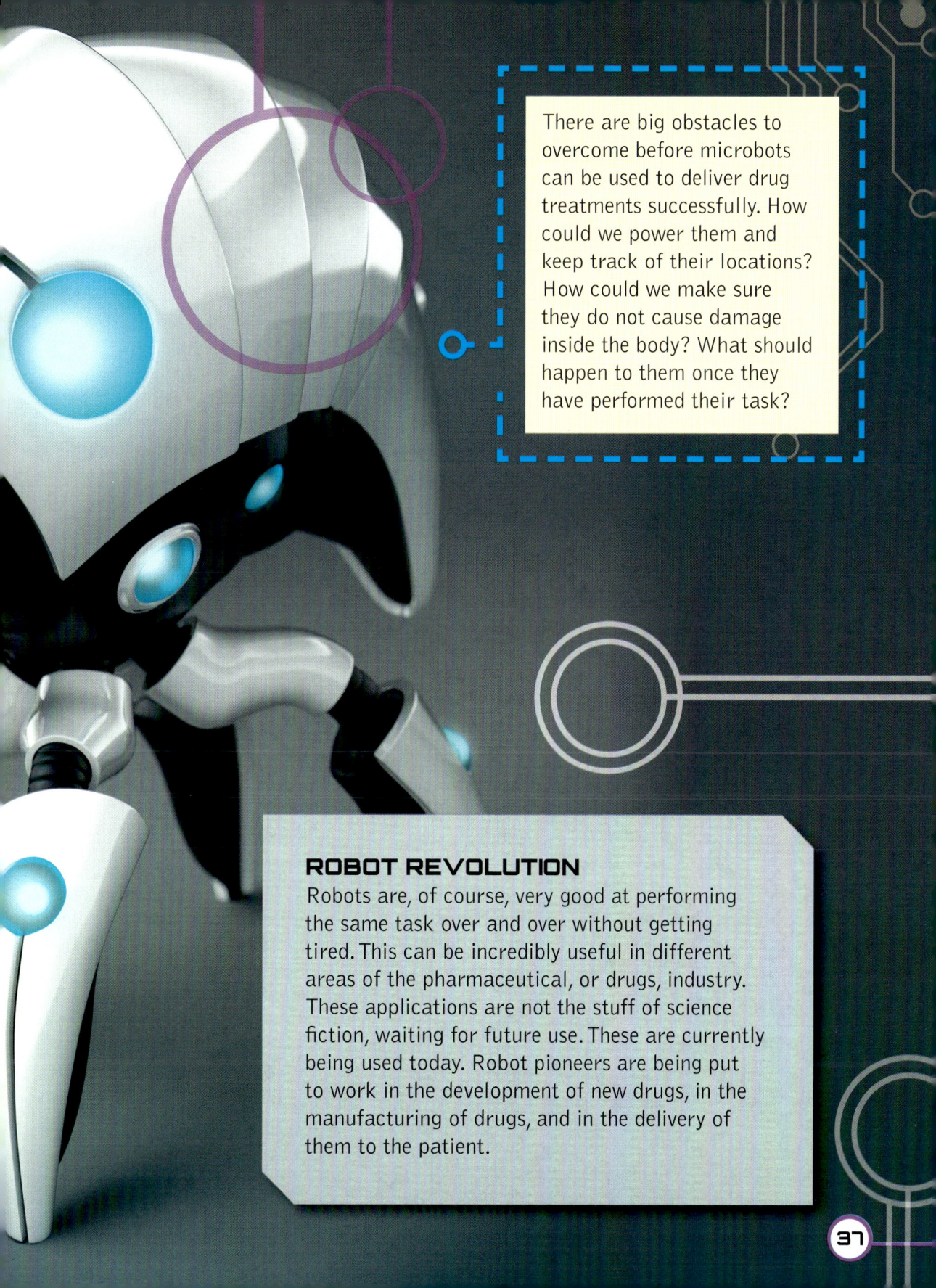

There are big obstacles to overcome before microbots can be used to deliver drug treatments successfully. How could we power them and keep track of their locations? How could we make sure they do not cause damage inside the body? What should happen to them once they have performed their task?

ROBOT REVOLUTION

Robots are, of course, very good at performing the same task over and over without getting tired. This can be incredibly useful in different areas of the pharmaceutical, or drugs, industry. These applications are not the stuff of science fiction, waiting for future use. These are currently being used today. Robot pioneers are being put to work in the development of new drugs, in the manufacturing of drugs, and in the delivery of them to the patient.

Cancer is one of the most widespread diseases around the world. Cancer develops when cells in the body that are not normal grow out of control and spread. A group of cancer cells is called a tumor. If part of a tumor breaks off, it can travel to a new location in the body and continue to grow. Tumors damage the healthy cells around them. This is why treatments for cancer target these rogue cells. First, a surgeon will try to remove the tumor, if possible. Secondly, drugs are given to kill any cancer cells remaining. The third main treatment is radiation. This is where the robots come in.

Hit the Target

Radiation therapy kills cancer cells. Radiation is delivered by powerful machines in rays that are aimed at the location of the tumor. The problem with radiation is that it also kills healthy cells around the tumor. It has side effects too, such as making the patient feel tired and nauseous.

It is important to give only as much radiation as is needed, and no more. A new robotic system of delivering radiation, called the CyberKnife, has proved very effective. It uses image guidance technology and robotic mobility to automatically track, detect, and correct the tumors with precisely guided, high-dose radiation. Because the doses of radiation are so precisely targeted, patients generally need fewer of them. The side effects are therefore reduced, so patients recover more quickly.

These breast cancer cells are dividing to form a tumor.

ROBOT REVOLUTION

Another great feature of the Cyberknife is that it can deliver radiation to areas of the body that cannot be reached by surgeons, because operating on them would cause too much damage to surrounding tissue. Tumors in the brain, the spine, and the lungs, for example, are very difficult to operate on. Cyberknife can target tumors such as these from any angle, killing the cancer cells without damaging surrounding areas.

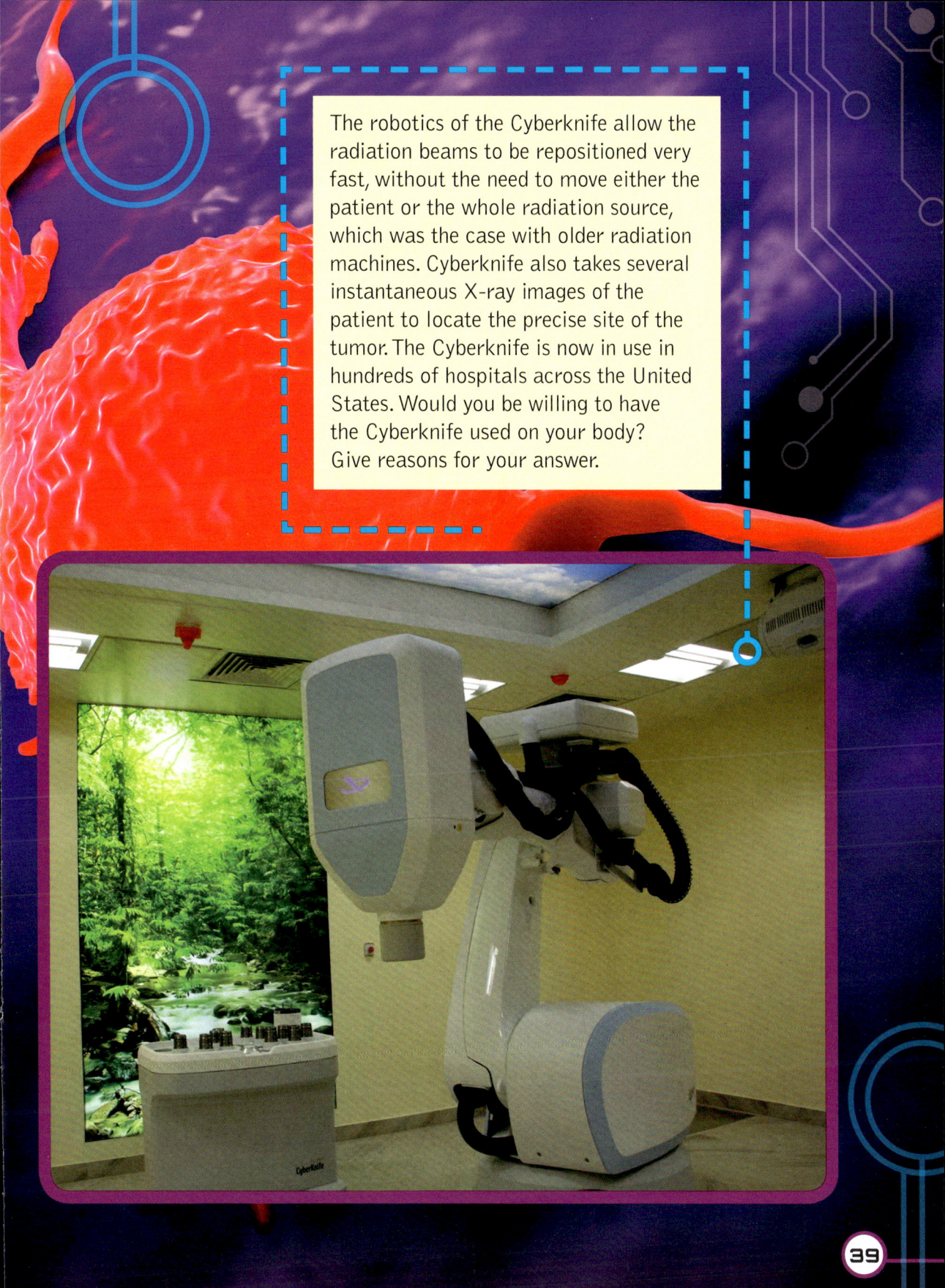

The robotics of the Cyberknife allow the radiation beams to be repositioned very fast, without the need to move either the patient or the whole radiation source, which was the case with older radiation machines. Cyberknife also takes several instantaneous X-ray images of the patient to locate the precise site of the tumor. The Cyberknife is now in use in hundreds of hospitals across the United States. Would you be willing to have the Cyberknife used on your body? Give reasons for your answer.

This automated hospital pharmacy is fast and accurate.

Pharmacies are places where drugs are dispensed, or given out. Every hospital has a pharmacy, where the pharmacists package up and give out medications that have been prescribed for patients by the doctors. In a busy, modern hospital, with many hundreds of patients, this is an incredibly complex task. Robots are now routinely used in this essential work, saving time and money.

Pharmabotics is the name for this pioneering area of robotic development. The automation begins immediately when the drugs are delivered to the hospital. They are tipped into a giant hopper, or container, then a conveyor belt moves them along to a machine that reads the barcodes on the packaging. Robotic arms then stack the boxes of medications onto shelves. The amazing thing is that the robot does this according to a system designed especially for it and known only by it. The robots know which drugs are used the most, and so organize the shelves accordingly, making the best use of the space available. This time-consuming task is the perfect job for an intelligent robot.

If pharmacists have more time to assess the needs of people who come in for their advice, that may save people a visit to their physician. How do you think this will help healthcare within the community?

A Joined Up System

Up on the wards, tablet computers have replaced pharmacists' prescription pads. The physician or nurse inputs an order, and the request goes instantly to the robot in the pharmacy. It selects and dispenses the medications. Nurses can check the progress of orders on a screen, which saves the time they used to spend going to the pharmacy or waiting for a medication delivery from the pharmacy technicians. Once the medications are dispensed, other robots can even deliver them around the hospital, to the wards where they were ordered.

Although pharmabots are expensive, hospitals say that they easily gain back more than the cost. This is because the system is more efficient, so they need to hold less stock at any one time. It is also more accurate.

Perhaps the biggest gain is in freeing up the time of skilled professionals to work with their patients. Some have worried that pharmacists will lose their jobs because of this automation, but pharmacists have a valuable role to play in interacting with patients. Pharmabots are beginning to appear in retail drugstores, too, dispensing medications to the general public.

In hospitals, medications are delivered to patients in several ways. Many people take pills, and we have seen how robots are helping to dispense these in an accurate, swift, and cost effective way. Other patients need treatment with fluid medications directly into their body, through a thin tube into their blood. This is called intravenous (IV) drug delivery. Here, too, robotics is playing a pioneering part.

With IV drug delivery it is vitally important to give the patient exactly the correct dose of medication. The drug is drip-fed into their veins over a period of hours, to be slowly absorbed by the body. One major use of IV medications is in the treatment of cancer, when it is known as chemotherapy. In repeated sessions over several months, the patient is given a combination of chemicals designed to kill the cancer cells in their tumor.

The common practice of mixing IV drugs by hand is time-consuming and open to mistakes. The chemicals are powerful, and also potentially dangerous for the staff handling them. There is also a risk that materials could become contaminated. A little more than 10 years ago, a medical equipment maker believed they could use robotic technology to prepare IV solutions reliably, and they set about the task. They created a robotic machine that works in a closed environment. This is important because it reduces the risk of the fluids being contaminated.

More Speed, Less Waste

Robotic IV delivery systems can make 40 to 60 doses of IV fluids per hour. Hospitals preparing IV fluids by hand traditionally made up batches of fluids once a day, but they may not have ended up using them all. This often resulted in a lot of fluids being wasted. Creating them to order, using the robot, is much less wasteful. This helps to offset the high cost of the robotic system. Improving the efficiency of drug delivery in this way allows the hospital's medical staff to spend more time with their patients, which is a major benefit.

IV fluids are delivered drop by drop into the patient's bloodstream.

This robotic machine prepares IV fluids autonomously and accurately.

ROBOT REVOLUTION
Robotic IV fluid machines use UV light to sterilize, or completely clean, the process, to avoid contamination. To produce the correct combinations of chemicals, they use barcode scanning, vision systems, and weight confirmation measures.

CHAPTER 6
TELEHEALTH

Medicine is all about bringing together skilled professionals with patients, to improve their health. Of course, generally people make an appointment to see their local doctor about a health concern, or they are admitted to the hospital to be treated for a more serious condition. As the demand for healthcare grows rapidly around the world, robotics are making an impact in medicine in this most fundamental way. They are managing to connect the patient with the clinician without the two even having to meet.

Around the world, billions of people live beyond the reach of conventional healthcare services because they are in remote locations. This can have a serious impact on their lives, especially in a medical emergency. Now, telehealth robotic networks are being created that allow top clinicians to conduct consults and treat patients many hundreds of miles away. If the patient is at home they can access the service on a tablet or computer. If they are in a clinic, they have even more options. The instruments used to examine the patient, for example, in their ears or throat, are linked into the telehealth network, so the specialist can see what the instrument sees, on their own screen in their hospital. They can then make a diagnosis and suggest treatment for the patient.

This doctor is talking to her patient remotely through her laptop.

This kind of consult has enormous potential to improve outcomes for patients. In the developed world a patient can be evaluated quickly in an emergency and a diagnosis made so that action can be taken swiftly. Speed is critical in emergency situations like these. For less urgent conditions, patients can be monitored regularly. The Remote Presence Virtual + Independent Telemedicine Assistant (RP-VITA) robot developed by InTouch Health and iRobot Corporation is being used in the United States to connect rural hospital systems to each other, to improve patient care in remote areas. It also supports medical services to prisons, where access to patients can be difficult.

There are many areas of medicine that can benefit from telehealth robotic networks. As well as acting quickly to save a patient's life in an emergency such as a stroke, they can identify infectious diseases. An epidemic of a disease such as influenza can spread quickly through a city, state, or country. If clinicians coordinate their information about patients from many hospitals in a telehealth network, they are more likely to spot an epidemic developing. How would telehealth networks like this help improve outcomes for patients?

Consultation, diagnosis, and treatment from a distance can greatly impact the quality of life of patients in isolated areas, where access to specialized medical services is limited. Despite this, across the world, billions of people cannot access safe surgery. To solve this problem, many more surgeons need to be trained. Robotics can take on an important role in this.

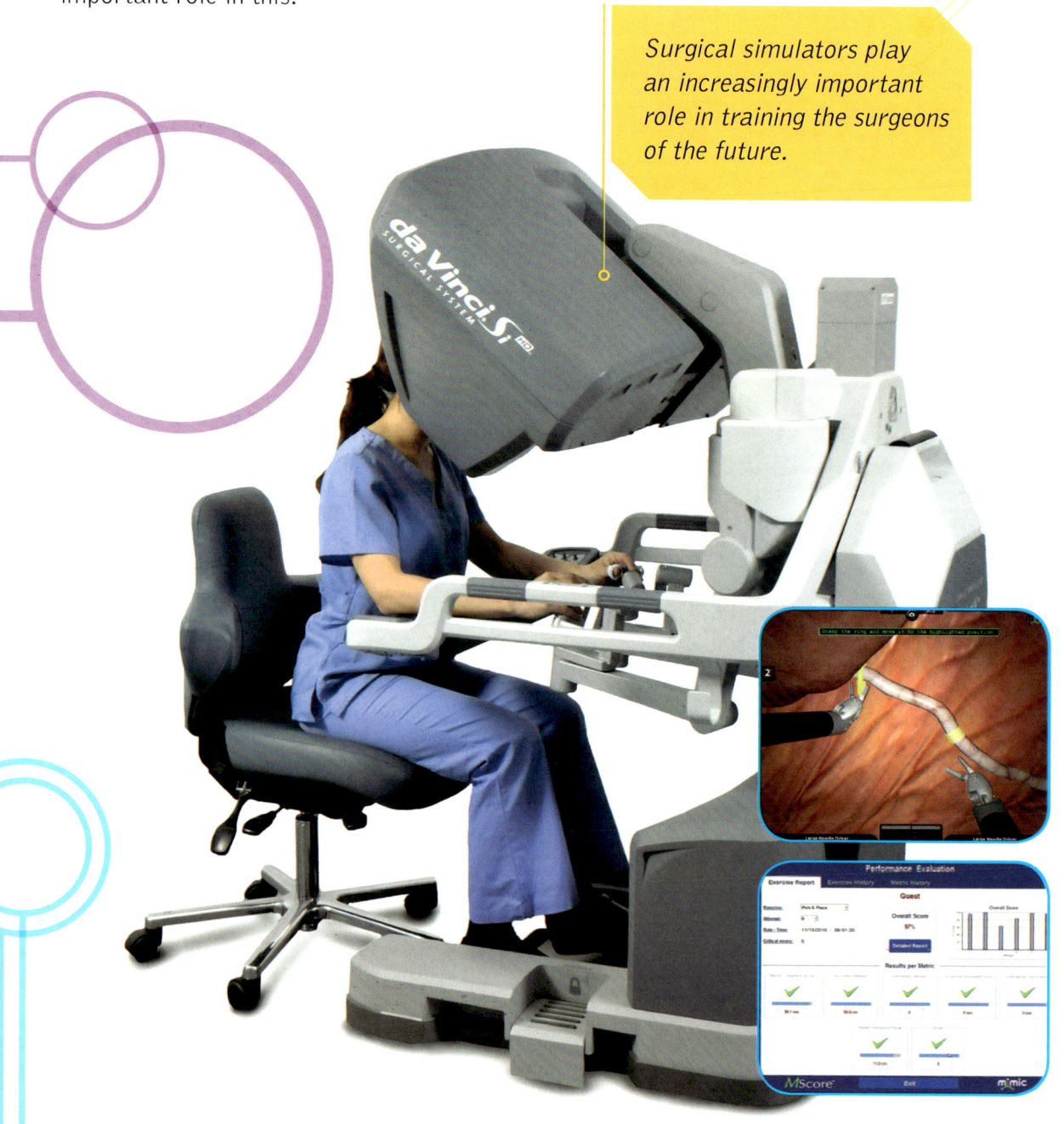

Surgical simulators play an increasingly important role in training the surgeons of the future.

Surgical Training

Surgery is a highly skilled process. It takes years to train a surgeon, and that is after they have already completed many years of medical school. Resident physicians work very long hours, which impacts the time they have for refining their skills. Advances in medicine are also introducing more and more new surgical procedures, techniques, and technologies, so they must keep up with learning these, too. They have less and less time for hands-on practice. The attending surgeons who train them are incredibly busy also. They have a full workload of surgeries, and less time to give to their students. The cost of them giving up surgery time to train their students is huge.

It takes at least 11 years to train as a surgeon in the United States.

Now, however, some people hope that virtual reality and robotics can revolutionize the way surgeons are trained. Instead of training in actual operating rooms, thousands of students could be learning at one time. Today, students around the world can watch real surgery being performed in one of the world's leading hospitals, over a network. This is valuable teaching, but they are not getting direct practice themselves. Researchers are working on the technology to allow them to actually use virtual robotic instruments, wherever they are. They would be able to feel the sensation of holding them, and of using them on a patient. Graphics and sound would add to the real-life experience.

ROBOT REVOLUTION

Another benefit of teletraining is that it is easier for the trainers to evaluate their students. The teacher can look at the student's work at a time to suit them. As the student and teacher do not meet, the process can be more objective. The machines should be able to evaluate the student's work using an accepted group of standards. This means that every student is being evaluated in the same way, which is a fairer way of doing it.

CHAPTER 7

RESEARCH AND DEVELOPMENT

The pace of change in medicine has never been faster. Around the world, researchers are developing new drugs, new procedures, and new treatments in the fight against disease. This work takes time, and often many people. While it needs the most expert and creative minds to find ways to push forward the frontiers of medicine, many of the processes involved in trialing and developing these innovations are very labor-intensive. This is where robots come in, as they are perfect for many of these jobs.

Over and Over

In a laboratory, robots are perfect for automating tasks that would be tedious, repetitive, or even hazardous for a person. Complex robots with dozens of "arms" can work with high volumes of samples at one time. The robots can sort, de-cap and re-cap test tubes, and load the tubes into machines called centrifuges where the samples are spun at high speed. They can safely handle substances that are poisonous or infectious, and they can operate in a sealed or climate-controlled area that people would find unbearable. They do not need to rest, or take vacations, and they never get sick.

Using robots in the laboratory has many clear advantages. There are some issues involved, too, however. These machines are expensive and complex. It takes a long time to design and set up a pioneering robotic system, and then to transfer from the old manual system. There is also a question of how well a robotic system can resolve a problem if an error occurs. However, once it is up and running, these systems can do in hours what once took days or weeks. Do you think they are a good thing? Give reasons for your answer.

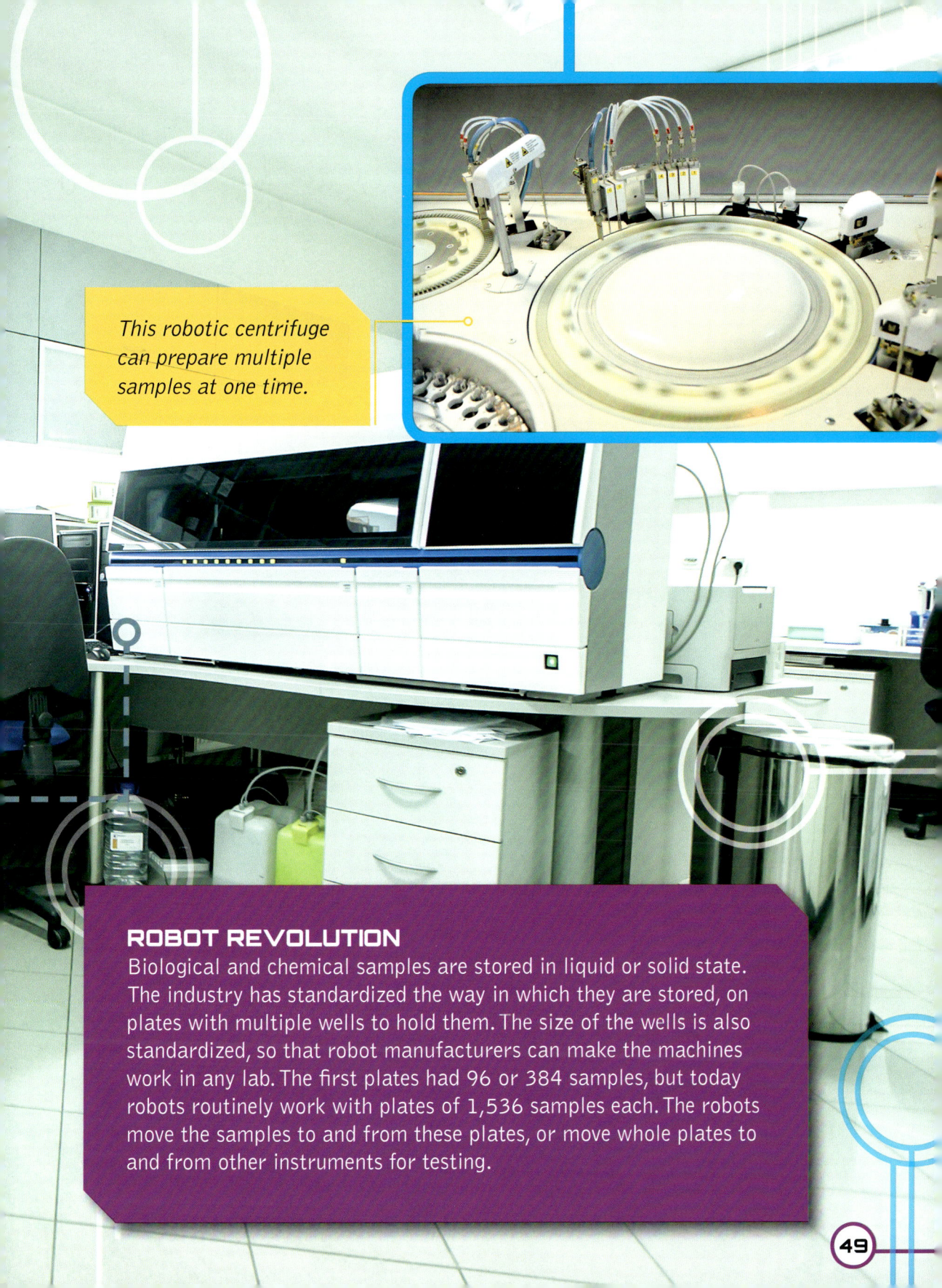

This robotic centrifuge can prepare multiple samples at one time.

ROBOT REVOLUTION

Biological and chemical samples are stored in liquid or solid state. The industry has standardized the way in which they are stored, on plates with multiple wells to hold them. The size of the wells is also standardized, so that robot manufacturers can make the machines work in any lab. The first plates had 96 or 384 samples, but today robots routinely work with plates of 1,536 samples each. The robots move the samples to and from these plates, or move whole plates to and from other instruments for testing.

Medicine needs drugs. Every day millions of people around the world take medications to improve their health. The pharmaceutical industry is one of the biggest in the world. It is constantly working to develop new drugs to provide better solutions to health problems. This is expensive and time-consuming work, but robots have become an essential part of it.

Volume and Content

Developing new drugs involves a lot of testing. Researchers decide which combinations of chemicals might work well together to treat a particular problem. They must try out many combinations, in differing quantities and in different conditions, to see what is most effective. At this basic level, robots can be used to prepare high volumes of samples for testing. Huge plates of samples are passed down an "assembly line" of processes. This is known as "high throughput screening" and robots have been doing it for many years. Hundreds of thousands of compounds can be tested in just a few hours.

This robot arm handles the plates of samples and transfers them from one testing process to the next.

This saves labor, but the costs are high and the success rate is relatively low. There is a lot of wastage of sample material. The robot does not bring any intelligence to this process. However, now developers are looking at ways to use them even more creatively. Processing the samples produces a huge amount of data. Each sample can produce 4 to 5 MB of data, even more if there are images included with it. Handling and managing this data is a big challenge, but it is perfect work for robots. What is even more exciting is that robots can be programmed to use this data and "learn" from it. They can use it to identify which samples are more likely to be successful, and only test those. This is known as "high content screening." It might narrow down the search for effective drug compounds, saving time and money.

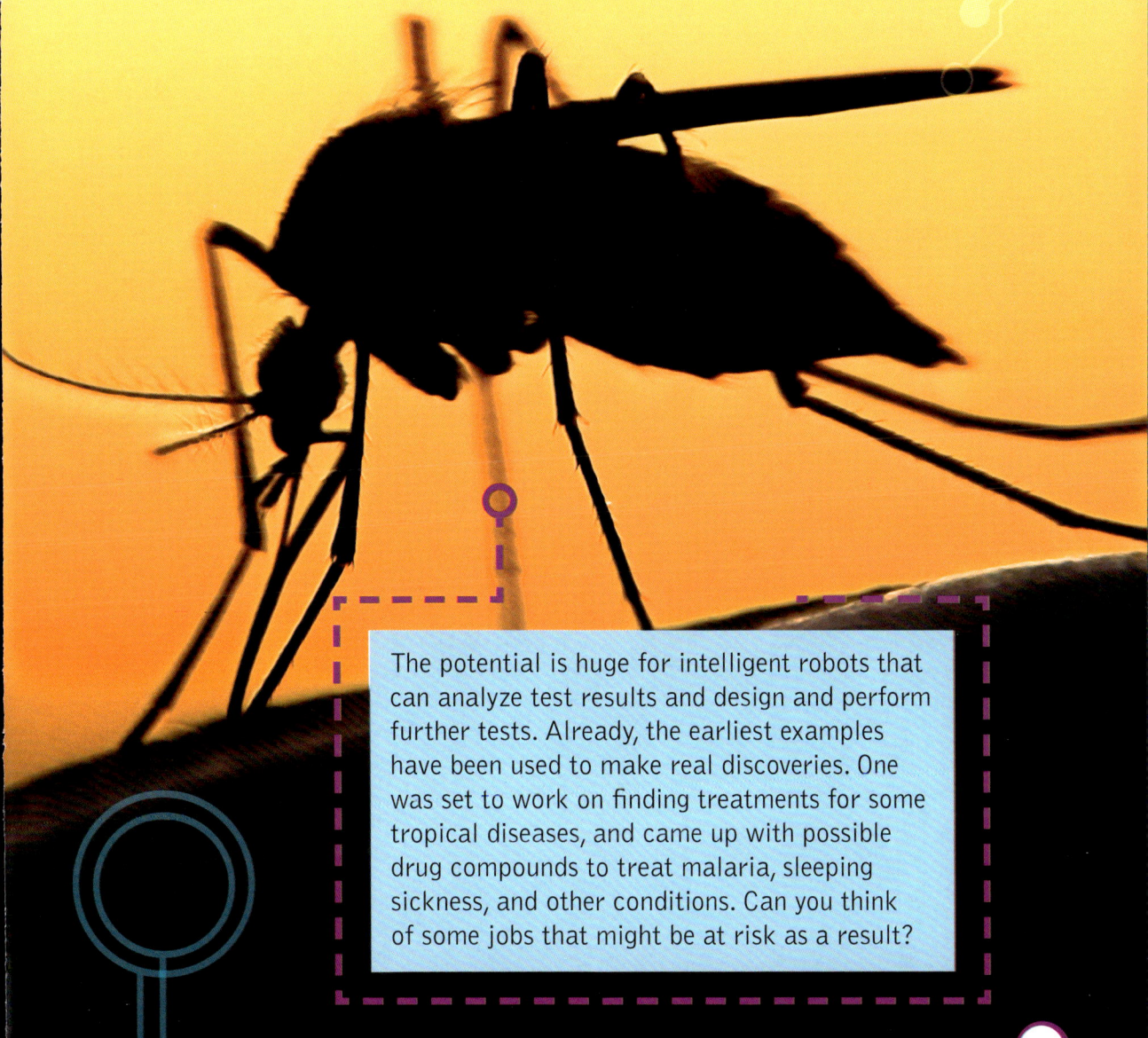

> The potential is huge for intelligent robots that can analyze test results and design and perform further tests. Already, the earliest examples have been used to make real discoveries. One was set to work on finding treatments for some tropical diseases, and came up with possible drug compounds to treat malaria, sleeping sickness, and other conditions. Can you think of some jobs that might be at risk as a result?

Modern medicine sometimes involves giving a patient an artificial device that will replace a part of the body that has stopped working properly. While in the past a failing heart or a broken hip might be life-threatening for a patient, today doctors can do so much to improve their chances of living a healthy life. There are many challenges in designing and making these artificial devices, but robotics is being put to work in this pioneering area of medicine.

Lifesavers

Thousands of people every year receive a new hip joint or knee joint. These joints often wear out as people become older, but younger patients can need them, too. Another device that patients receive is a pacemaker. This small object is implanted in the chest. It uses electricity from a battery to stimulate the heart muscle, and regulate its beating so that it can pump the blood around the body effectively. Millions of people with heart disease have received one of these since they were invented in the 1950s.

Implanting objects like these devices into the body is risky. The body is designed to reject "foreign" objects. The materials the devices are made of must be carefully chosen, they must be precisely made, and they must be absolutely clean and free of infection when they enter the body. Robotics are now being used to make these devices, which can be customized to fit the patient exactly. Physicians and engineers are working together to tailor replacements for hips, knees, shoulders, elbows, and even fingers that perform as much like the real thing as possible.

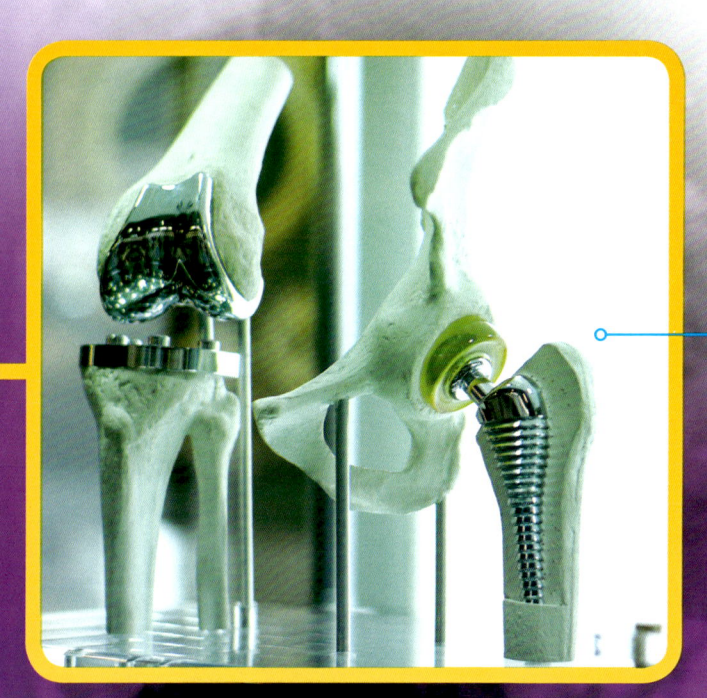

Artificial knee (left) and hip (right) joints need to be made with great precision.

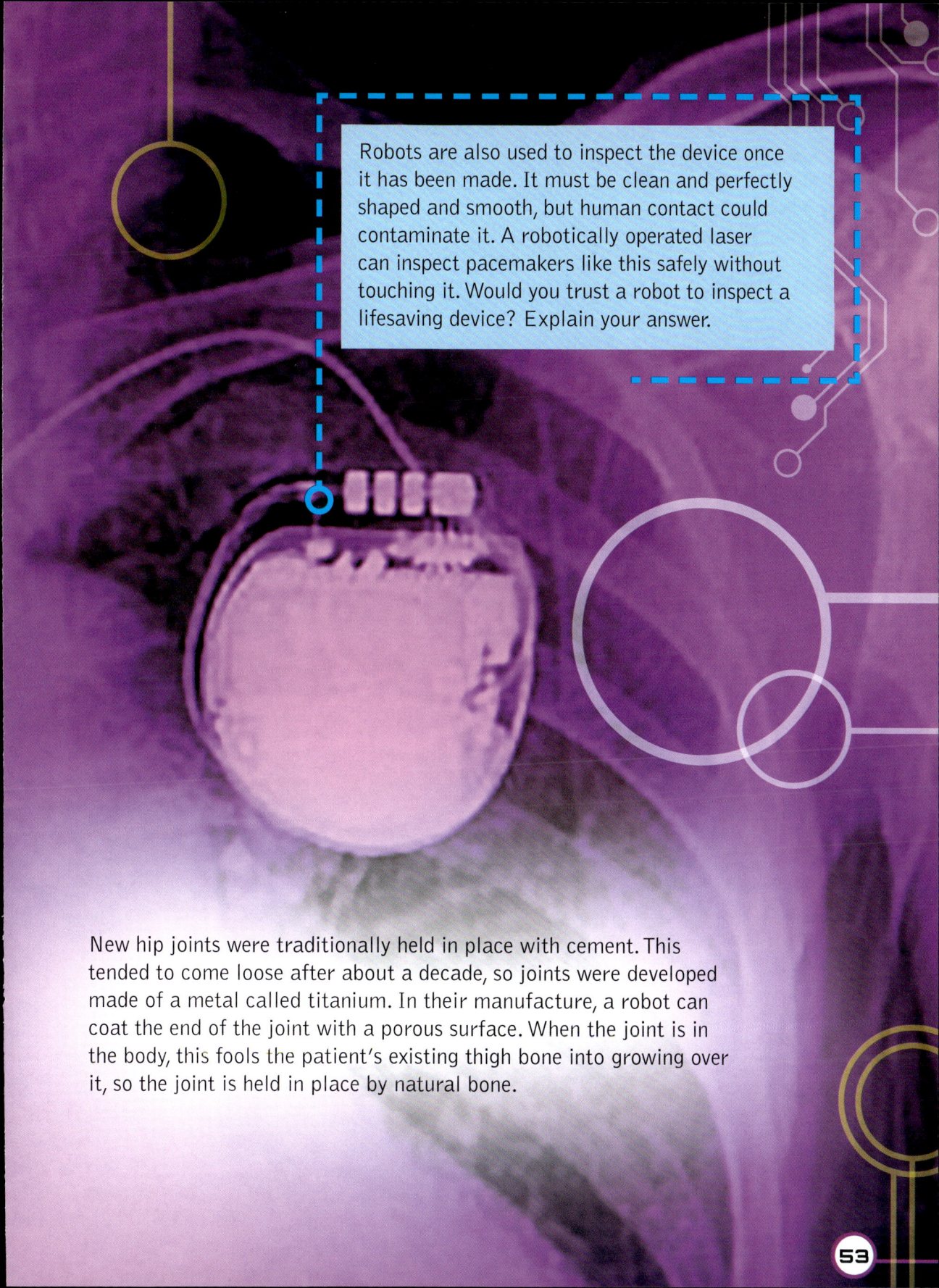

Robots are also used to inspect the device once it has been made. It must be clean and perfectly shaped and smooth, but human contact could contaminate it. A robotically operated laser can inspect pacemakers like this safely without touching it. Would you trust a robot to inspect a lifesaving device? Explain your answer.

New hip joints were traditionally held in place with cement. This tended to come loose after about a decade, so joints were developed made of a metal called titanium. In their manufacture, a robot can coat the end of the joint with a porous surface. When the joint is in the body, this fools the patient's existing thigh bone into growing over it, so the joint is held in place by natural bone.

CHAPTER 8
THE FUTURE

There is no doubt that the potential for robots in medicine in the future is enormous and far reaching. This exciting area, where engineering is meeting science, is generating some extraordinary technology. The pace of change is so fast that it is hard to say exactly what robots may be doing for people in 20 years' time, but they are sure to be an integral part of society.

Smaller and Smaller
Microbots are small enough to operate inside the human body, delivering drugs to targeted locations. One recent scientific advance is making the production even easier, and that is 3D printing. This enables it to be precisely styled for its function, and easily reproducible too. Nanobots are even smaller robots, and these promise equally amazing treatments. Nanobots are small enough to be injected into a patient's blood and travel around the body. It can be used to detect infections from bacteria and viruses, and even help to find cancer cells. Once it has found these, it can invade and destroy the cells. It acts like an extra army, together with the body's own white blood cells, in the fight against infection.

This illustration shows how a nanobot could look locating a cell.

Nanobots are being used in dentistry to deliver anesthetics to the patient before a procedure. It acts fast, and wears off more quickly, perfect for patients who do not like needles. They can also detect sensitive teeth, and numb the nerves to stop the pain permanently. It is even possible they could be used to directly manipulate the tissues in the jaw, to reposition and straighten teeth in minutes or hours. Could this be the end of having to wear braces for months?

Using nanobots to attack cancer cells has fewer harmful side effects for the patient than the traditional treatments of chemotherapy and radiotherapy, which can cause sickness, hair loss, and fatigue. It is a promising possible treatment for cancers in an early stage of growth. This most pioneering technology is incredibly exciting, with many other possible applications.

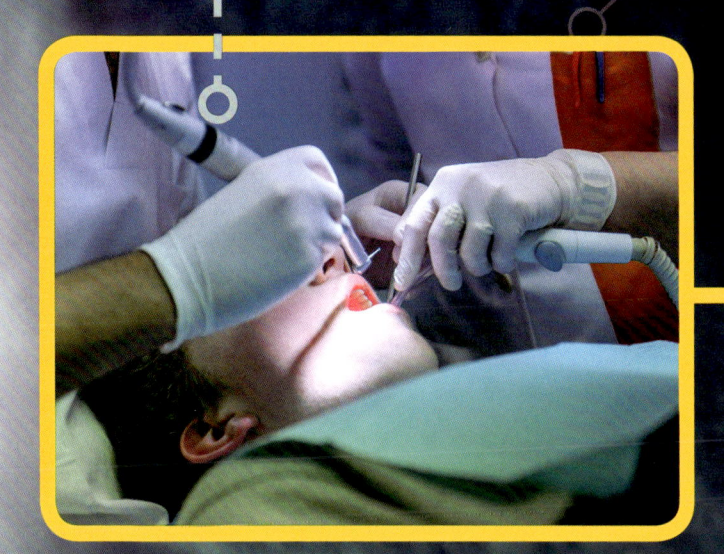

ROBOT REVOLUTION
On a different scale, robotics engineers are also working on improving replacement limbs for patients. A newly developed touch-sensitive artificial skin could mean that future artificial limbs will be able to "feel" just like real ones. It can detect pressure, and send back signals to a host "nerve center." The wearer could feel different textures, and distinguish between hot and cold.

Everyone involved in the development of surgical robots expects that their technical capabilities will continue to improve in the future. Robots already play an important part in some areas of surgery, but could the role of the expert surgeon be under threat?

One exciting new development in surgical robotics is in treatments for heart disease. This long-term condition affects millions of people, and it gradually becomes worse as the patient ages. Scientists in the United States have developed a robotic sleeve that can help hearts to pump when they are failing. It is made of a silicone-like material that acts like heart muscle. It hugs the outside of the heart and squeezes it when inflated with pressurized air. So far it has only been tested on pig hearts, but the results are promising. The body is less likely to reject this device than one that is implanted inside the heart. The most drastic treatment for heart disease is a heart transplant, but donor hearts are in short supply. This robotic device may in the future offer hope for patients with this life-threatening condition.

Real-Life Experience

Surgical robots like the da Vinci system can help to minimize the trauma to the patient, and improve their recovery time. So far, however, these tools cannot tell the difference between healthy tissue and cancer cells, for example. They cannot "feel" the tissue to judge how hard or soft it is. Engineers are working on developing ways for the surgeon operating with these surgical tools to have an experience much more like the one of open surgery, which involves standing over the patient.

In heart disease, fatty deposits build up in the coronary arteries, the blood vessels that supply the heart.

Surgery requires more than just precision in performing a procedure. Surgeons use their judgment every day to decide whether or not surgery is right for a patient, and to make decisions in response to events that occur in the operating room. A robot cannot have the surgeon's detailed knowledge of the human body, built up over years of experience. It also cannot interact with the patient as a person. What it can do is be a useful tool in the surgeon's hand, helping them to use all their talents as well as possible. Are there any ways in which a robot could perform better than a human surgeon?

The most pioneering developments in robotics for medicine are in making them more "intelligent." Robots are already useful tools for performing repetitive tasks, or tasks that could be hazardous for a human. A robot can reach parts of the body that other tools cannot reach. In the future, perhaps robots will be able to use their powers to learn lessons that could help physicians.

In fact, this is beginning to happen. Some robots have used their artificial intelligence to predict when patients with a heart disorder will die. The patients had high blood pressure in the lungs. This damages part of the heart, and about one-third of patients die within five years of being diagnosed. Doctors need to know the patient's chances of survival before they decide on the best treatment to give them.

The robots were given the results of a lot of different tests, including scans of the patients' hearts, blood tests, and their health records over eight years. They also measured the movement of 30,000 different points in the heart during each heartbeat. The machines learned which abnormalities in the heart predicted when the patients would die. The robots correctly predicted those who would still be alive after one year about 80 percent of the time. Doctors get it right about 60 percent of the time. This artificial intelligence could allow doctors to spot the patients most at risk, and give them the most appropriate treatment. It could also be used to diagnose different kinds of heart failure.

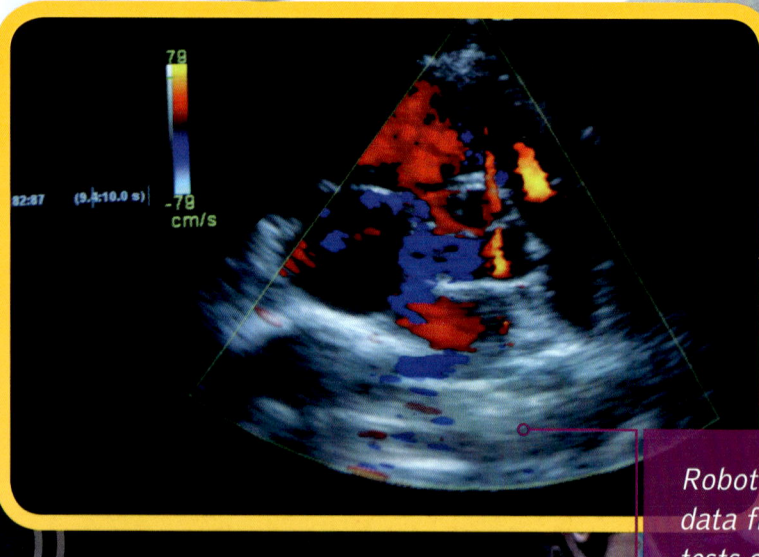

Robotics combined with data from scans and other tests could help doctors predict and prevent more heart disease.

There has been much debate about how far robots should be able to work autonomously, meaning without input from a person. There are obvious safety issues around robots working unsupervised, and the regulators work hard only to authorize robots that can operate safely under human supervision. A network of robots, however, could spread their abilities across a wider area, bringing benefit to more physicians and patients. How could humans monitor a network of robots?

A Powerful Network

At the moment, robots generally work independently of one another. They are set up in a particular situation to perform a particular task. If they could be connected, a series of robots could share their intelligence. This could improve their effectiveness, and open up new areas for development.

Robots are already at work in the world of medicine, and these machines have huge potential for the future. Robots are being put to good use in training medical practitioners, helping with surgery and rehab, with research, and with drug development.

How Far Is Too Far?

Is there a limit to what robots could, or should do in medicine? With all its scientific sophistication, medicine still centers on one person—the doctor, surgeon, nurse, or therapist—interacting with another person, the patient, who is in trouble. These human relationships are important, and they are a vital part of the medic's role. Patients must trust the people taking care of them, and believe they are in safe hands. If the processes of medicine are automated too far, it is possible that the patient will not accept them, or will feel alienated and anxious. How we feel plays a big part in how well we recover.

Robotic probes help doctors see the most inaccessible areas of the body.

ROBOT REVOLUTION

The latest developments in robotics for surgery are focused on making devices that are smaller, lighter, and easier for the surgeon to control. These machines are designed to enhance the way surgeries are done, rather than change it dramatically, for example, by giving the surgeon access to areas of the body that cannot be reached by hands. The devices have more artificial intelligence, but remain very much in the surgeon's control.

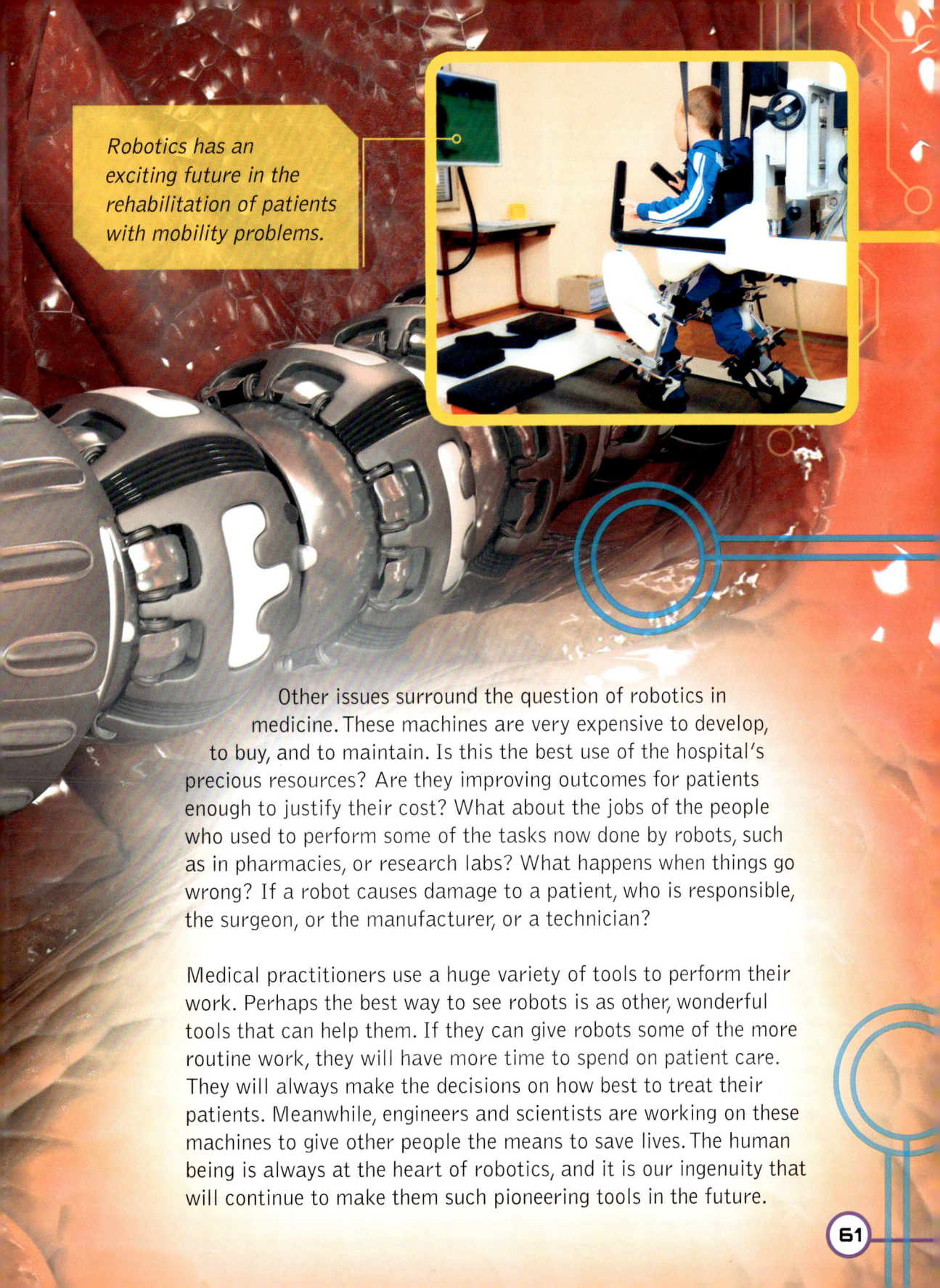

Robotics has an exciting future in the rehabilitation of patients with mobility problems.

Other issues surround the question of robotics in medicine. These machines are very expensive to develop, to buy, and to maintain. Is this the best use of the hospital's precious resources? Are they improving outcomes for patients enough to justify their cost? What about the jobs of the people who used to perform some of the tasks now done by robots, such as in pharmacies, or research labs? What happens when things go wrong? If a robot causes damage to a patient, who is responsible, the surgeon, or the manufacturer, or a technician?

Medical practitioners use a huge variety of tools to perform their work. Perhaps the best way to see robots is as other, wonderful tools that can help them. If they can give robots some of the more routine work, they will have more time to spend on patient care. They will always make the decisions on how best to treat their patients. Meanwhile, engineers and scientists are working on these machines to give other people the means to save lives. The human being is always at the heart of robotics, and it is our ingenuity that will continue to make them such pioneering tools in the future.

GLOSSARY

algorithms Sets of rules for solving a problem.
anatomy The structure of the body.
android A robot that looks like a human being.
antibiotics Substances that destroy bacteria.
artificial intelligence The ability of a machine to perform tasks that normally require human intelligence, such as understanding speech.
assembly line A series of machines that build an object, such as a car.
autonomous Able to act independently.
bacteria Tiny organisms that can cause disease.
cosmetic surgery Surgery to change the appearance of part of the body.
dementia An illness of the brain where people lose their mental capacity.
dexterity Skill in performing a task, generally using the hands.
DNA The substance in our cells that stores the information that defines who we are.
epidemic An outbreak of a disease that spreads fast across a wide area.
exoskeleton A powered walking aid that a patient wears on their body.
follicle The part of the structure of a hair that is under the skin.
intravenous Into a vein.
invasive Something that involves the introduction of medical instruments into the body.
malaria A disease caught from mosquito bites.
microbots Small robots, generally less than 0.004 in (1 mm) across.
microsurgery Surgery performed using miniature instruments and a microscope.
nanobots Very small robots, generally less than 0.00004 in (1 micrometer) across.
orthopedic The treatment of bones and muscles.
pacemaker A medical device implanted in the body to regulate the way the heart beats.
pharmabotics The use of robotics in the pharmaceutical industry.
pharmaceutical The industry that develops and manufactures medications.
physiotherapists Medical practitioners who use exercises and massage to improve a patient's mobility.
porous Allowing liquid or air to pass through.
radiation A form of energy used in the treatment of cancer.
stroke A condition during which blood supply to the brain is cut off.
suturing Sewing up tissue during surgery using stitches.
transplant The transfer of a part of the body, such as a heart or lung, from one person to another to save the recipient's life.
tumors Groups of cancer cells.
ultraviolet (UV) light A kind of light, beyond the range of colors we can see.
viruses Tiny organisms that can cause disease.
white blood cells Cells that fight infection.

FOR MORE INFORMATION

Books

Koontz, Robin. *Robotics in the Real World*.
Minneapolis, MN: Core Library, 2016.

Mooney, Carla. *Wearable Robots*.
Chicago, IL: Norwood House Press, 2016.

Spilsbury, Louise. *Robots in Medicine*.
New York, NY: Gareth Stevens, 2015.

Swanson, Jennifer. *National Geographic Kids Everything Robotics: All the Photos, Facts, and Fun to Make You Race for Robots*.
Des Moines, IA: National Geographic, 2016.

Websites

Learn all about the human body at:
www.easyscienceforkids.com/human-body

Discover all there is to know about the cute, cuddly Paro robot:
www.parorobots.com

Follow these fun step-by-step instructions to build your own simple robots:
www.sciencebuddies.org/robot-projects

Click through the pages to find out how robots work:
www.science.howstuffworks.com/robot.htm

Publisher's note to educators and parents: Our editors have carefully reviewed these websites to ensure that they are suitable for students. Many websites change frequently, however, and we cannot guarantee that a site's future contents will continue to meet our high standards of quality and educational value. Be advised that students should be closely supervised whenever they access the Internet.

INDEX

A
android robots, 7, 30
animal robots, 34–35
arm supports, 27
ARTAS™ System, 22, 23
artificial devices, 52–53
artificial intelligence, 23, 34, 58–59, 60
artificial skin, 55
attachments, 17
autonomous robots, 5, 18–20, 26–27, 40–41, 43, 59

B
bone surgery, 12–14

C
cameras, 18, 21
cancer treatment, 16, 38–39, 42, 54–56
cognitive therapy robot pets, 34
complications, 15
consoles, 14, 16
cosmetic surgery, 22–23
cost of robots, 16, 19, 41, 61
Cyberknife, 38–39

D
da Vinci system, 14–17, 46, 56
data collection, 30, 31, 33
data management, 51
dentistry, 7, 55
difficult-to-reach body areas, 20–21, 38, 58, 60
dispensing medicine, 4, 40–41
drug delivery, 36–37
drug development and testing, 50–51
dummy robots, 6

E
elderly patients, 29, 30, 32, 33, 34
emotional support, 34
epidemics, 45
exoskeletons, 24–25
eye surgery, 10–11

F
Flex®, 20–21

H
hair transplant surgery, 22–23

HAL (Hybrid Assistive Limb) for Care Support, 28–30
heart disease, 16, 52, 56, 58
high content screening, 51
human help, 19, 23
human operators, 5, 12, 30, 59

I
infection control, 8–9
interacting with patients, 7, 30, 34–35, 41, 57, 60
intravenous (IV) drug delivery, 42–43
IPAM robot, 26
isolated patients, 44, 46

J
joints, artificial, 13, 52–53

K
keyhole surgery, 10, 16

L
laboratory robots, 48–49
lifting patients, 28–29
limb replacements, 55

M
microbots, 36–37
microsurgery, 11
mobility robots, 24–25, 61

N
nanobots, 54–55
networking robots, 59
Nursebots, 32–33
nurses, 28–33

O
orthopedic surgery, 12–14

P
pacemakers, 52–53
Paro seal pup robot, 34–35
Pearl robot, 32–33
pharmabotics, 40–43
pharmacies, 4, 40–43
physiotherapy, 26–27
precise movements, 10–11, 13, 14, 15
predicting disease, 58
probes, 60

R
real-life simulation robots, 7
reducing side effects, 36, 38
reducing strain, 16
reducing stress, 29
reducing tissue damage, 13
rehabilitation, 24, 27, 61
Renaissance robot, 12
research and development, 48–53
research labs, 4, 48–51
Robear robot, 30
RP-VITA, 45

S
safety issues, 15, 27, 59
samples, working with, 48–51
scans, 12–13, 58
scoliosis surgery, 13
sensors, 7, 24, 29, 30
Simroid, 7
smaller incisions, 10, 12–13, 15
soft tissue surgery, 14, 19
spinal surgery, 12–13
STAR (Smart Tissues Autonomous Robot), 18–19
Steady-Hand Eye Robot, 11
steadiness, 11
surgery, 10–23, 47, 56–57, 60
suturing, 18–19

T
targeting treatment, 38–39
telehealth, 33, 44–47
Terapio robot, 30–31
training dentists, 7
training students, 6–7, 47
training surgeons, 17, 46–47
TSolution One, 13

U
UV light robots, 9, 43

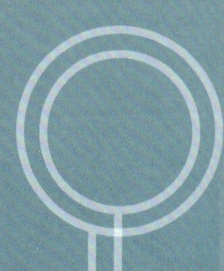

64